Cubase VST

tricks

Ian Waugh

PC Publishing
Export House
130 Vale Road
Tonbridge
Kent TN9 1SP
UK

Tel 01732 770893
Fax 01732 770268
email info@pc-publishing.co.uk
web site http://www.pc-publishing.co.uk

First published 1999

© PC Publishing
An imprint of Music Technology Books Limited

ISBN 1 870775 63 5

British Library Cataloguing in Publication Data
A catalogue record for this book is available from the British Library

Printed by Bell and Bain Ltd., Glasgow

Contents

Dedication

To my parents for understanding why I couldn't always be there...
To Pam and Ted for understanding why I couldn't always phone...
But most of all

   To Julia for understanding ...

With much love

Introduction

Cubase VST! It's big. It's versatile. It's incredibly powerful. It can seem complex. Are you sure you're getting the most out of it?

This book is a collection of hints and tips designed to help you do just that. It's not a substitute for the manual; it's not a VST instruction book.

The hints and tips cover a wide range of topics and you may want to check out first those areas that you use the most. But do check out the tips for the features you rarely use, too – you never know when one will spark an interesting musical idea.

Although you will get more from this book if you read all of it – and you do want to get your money's worth, don't you? – you can dip into it and read the tips in any order you wish.

But do, do, do please read the first chapter on setting up. This explains how to optimise your computer and VST in order to get the maximum performance out of your system. Digital audio and real-time effects make great demands on your computer's processing power and until we're all sitting snugly with 2000MHz machines you need to make the most of the (limited) power you have. (If you are sitting with a 2000MHz machine, this book is probably a valuable antique and don't you wish you'd bought two copies?)

And if you're working with digital audio, do read the second chapter about hard disks, too.

As you know, Cubase VST is a cross-platform application, available for both Mac and PC. The majority of the tips in this book are applicable to both Mac and PC versions of the program. Where this is not the case, any differences are clearly indicated.

As of writing, there are three versions of the program – Cubase VST, Cubase VST Score and Cubase VST/24. The core functions of all three programs are the same. Score and VST/24 have enhanced score layout functions while VST/24 has extended support for digital audio hardware.

Version 4 of the program was the most major upgrade to Cubase since VST and this is the version on which this book is based. Most of the tips ought to work with earlier versions unless, of course, a specific feature was introduced with version 4. Sometimes there is a reference to v4 in the text, possibly with a comment about how to perform a similar function with an earlier version but if you can't a find a feature in your copy of VST, you may need an upgrade!

Finally, the tips and tricks in this book are intended to help you get more out of Cubase VST. Although some of them are neat and cute, don't lose sight of the fact that the reason you use VST is to make music and that should always be your overriding purpose.

Setting up

This is one of the most important chapters in the book. If you don't read any of the others, read this!

Gone are the days when you could simply boot up a sequencer and start using it without making any technical adjustments to the equipment. There are now so many different types of PC and Mac, so many different types of sound card, so many potential ways of impairing a program's performance that you need to optimise your computer system to make sure that VST is running as efficiently as possible.

Failure to do so could result in any number of problems. It could be something as 'simple' as not running VST to its full potential – it may not play as many audio Tracks or process as many real-time effects as possible. It may seem to work okay but it would be like driving a car in third gear. However, the problems could be much more serious, such as audio dropouts or the audio and MIDI data running out of sync.

If you have already experienced problems with VST, hopefully some of the suggestions in this chapter and in the Troubleshooting chapters should help you put things right.

On the other hand, you may have installed VST, discovered that it works just fine and decided all's well with the world. It could be, but you may also be able to improve its performance by the judicious tweaking of a few parameters.

Keep up to date

Cubase VST is in a continual state of development. Steinberg is constantly looking for ways to improve and add to the program, hence the once- or twice-yearly updates which we rush out to buy.

However, the company also releases smaller updates which may add some small new function, improve the program's performance and, dare we say, fix the odd bug. It is always, therefore, a good idea to check for these updates which may fix problems or improve performance. They are always available on Steinberg's Web site, Figure 1.1, and this ought to be your first stop:

http://www.steinberg.de

From here you can access sites and download areas in other parts of the world. Any other sites or sub-sites Steinberg may develop will be accessible from here, too.

Figure 1.1 The Steinberg Web site is an essential source of information and should be bookmarked

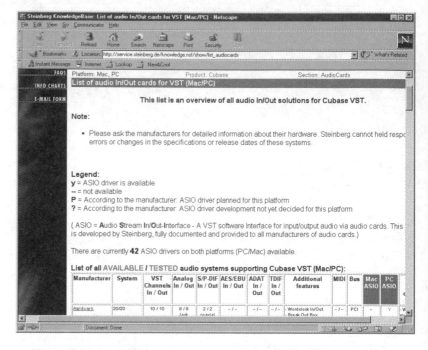

If you don't have Web access, keep in touch with the technical support department of your local distributor. It's generally little use making friends with the guys and gals in your local music shop – unless one of them owns a record company or has a cute sister or brother – or unless you genuinely like them, of course! Unless they are active users of VST or keep up to date with developments on the Web, they are most unlikely to know about such updates. Nothing personal; they have enough to do keeping up with the new gear arriving in the shop without trying to keep track of the incremental updates all the software developers keep releasing.

On-line help

It has been known for the odd incremental update to bring its own problems so always make sure you can revert to the previous installation before updating your program.

A good way to discover the benefits – and potential problems – of the upgrades is to join the musical on-line community. There are several newsgroups and mailing lists for the musician including at least one for Cubase users: alt.steinberg.cubase. Many on-line communities such as AOL, CompuServe and Cix also have dedicated music and Cubase areas which can be an invaluable source of help and knowledge.

Accessing newsgroups and joining mailing lists is beyond the scope of this book (it's not at all difficult to do, just a little involved) but your ISP (Internet Service Provider) ought to be able help. There are also, of course, copious amounts of information about newsgroups and mailing lists on the Net itself and, if you will permit a small gratuitous promotion, you can find out more about them and how to use them in the book, *Music on the Internet (and where to find it)* which should be available from wherever you got this book. They are both published by PC Publishing.

✦ **INFO** ✦

You can phone PC Publishing on 01732 770893 or fax 01732 770268. Their Web site is at: www.pc-publishing.co.uk

Sound card set-up

For high quality audio you need a high quality sound card, although on the PC VST should work with any MME-compatible card including 'consumer' cards. Most PCI audio cards will work on the Mac providing suitable Mac drivers are available. VST/24 supports 24-bit cards and 24-bit recording is rapidly becoming the recording resolution of choice – until 32-bit takes over!

All sound cards are not equal. Steinberg has helpfully posted a list of VST-compatible cards on its Web site. As of writing it is accessible through the KnowledgeBase section of the site although I won't give the URL as it is subject to change. The list includes basic feature information about the cards, tells you if ASIO drivers are available for Mac and PC or whether they are in development.

ASIO allows manufacturers to write dedicated drivers for their hardware which bypass the traditional operating system, reducing latency.

INFO

ASIO – Audio Stream In/Out technology. A software interface which communicates between music software such as VST and hardware such as audio cards.

ASIO 2

Although ASIO works well, Steinberg has released details of ASIO 2 which improves several areas of performance and functionality. It has enhanced sync options which allows sample-accurate positioning. ASIO 1 handled the synchronization of data across various outputs but absolute positioning was provided by MTC (MIDI Time Code). This works fine in most situations but when transferring data from an ADAT device the positioning was effectively quantized to the nearest quarter frame (one frame equals 1/75th of a second). ASIO 2 includes a protocol to define the absolute time to ensure sample-accurate synchronization.

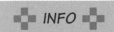

INFO

Latency – the response time or the length of time it takes a system to react to a signal. With digital audio it's the delay between playing a sound and hearing it.

ASIO 2 also enables several ASIO applications to run at the same time and share the audio output. With ASIO 1, the first application would grab the audio hardware making it unavailable to any other application. With ASIO 2, as you switch between applications, the ASIO control is switched, too.

A major new feature with ASIO 2 is Direct Monitoring. Standard drivers typically have a 750 millisecond latency in Windows which means a considerable delay between inputting or playing a sound and hearing or monitoring it. A well-written ASIO driver can reduce that to 40 milliseconds or less. However, ASIO 2 allows any ASIO input to be directly assigned to any ASIO output when using the record monitor function, which Steinberg claims reduces the latency to zero.

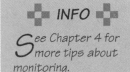

INFO

See Chapter 4 for more tips about monitoring.

For an application to benefit from these features, both the host application and the hardware need to conform to ASIO 2. You should find most drivers and ASIO applications supporting ASIO 2 throughout 1999 and into the Millennium by which time all software and hardware should be ASIO 2-compliant. But do check before you buy. As of writing, cards scheduled for ASIO 2 drivers include the Lexicon Studio; Digidesign D24, Event's Layla, Gina and Darla; MotU's 2408; Korg 1212I/O; and Sonorus StudI/O. Doubtless if ASIO drivers are to be written for any cards they will be ASIO 2.

Which drivers to use and when

If your sound card has a dedicated ASIO driver (that is, one written specifically for the card), use this by preference. Otherwise, use the DirectX ASIO driver or the ASIO Multimedia driver, Figure 1.2. The drivers, used in that order, will give better performance in terms of lower latency.

Figure 1.2 ASIO drivers are selected in the Audio System Setup dialog

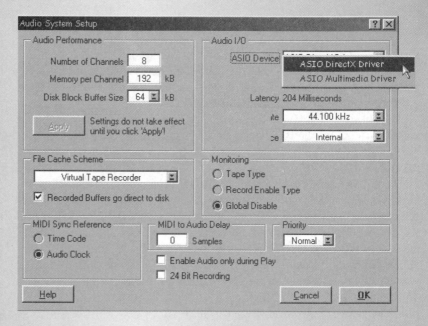

A DirectX driver will enable you to run VST with a soft synth, for example. Note, however, that it currently only supports audio playback, not recording (because Microsoft DirectX itself only supports audio output, not input).

Use ASIO DirectX

• When you only need to playback, not record
• When you do not need several audio outputs
• When you want to play audio from two or more applications (assuming they all support DirectX)

Use ASIO Multimedia

• For recording
• If you don't have a problem with the higher latency during playback

Use the latest drivers

Whichever platform and sound card you use, check the manufacturer's Web site regularly to make sure you have the latest drivers. This is particularly important if the card is a new model as 'quirks' often show up which are cured by new drivers.

Set the sync

If you have more than one audio device, you need to select the one to be used for the Sync Reference. In the System Setup window, open the ASIO Multimedia Panel, select the audio device you want to use and move it to the top of the list with the Move up button, Figure 1.3.

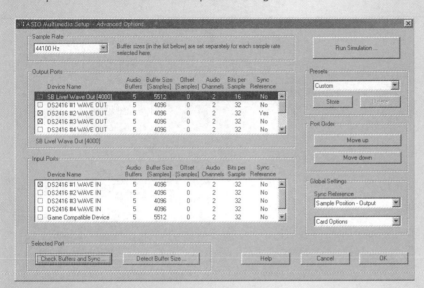

Figure 1.3 The audio device used for the Sync Reference should be on the top of the list

Sample Position vs. DMA Block

The Sync Reference in the Global Settings area of the Advanced Options window, Figure 1.4, is used to synchronize MIDI playback to the audio.

   To achieve the best possible synchronization and timing, use Sample Position. In this mode, the number of samples being played is passed to VST and used to synchronize MIDI playback. It is the equivalent of synchronizing to a sample-accurate clock.

   In DMA Block mode, the transfer of blocks of data by DMA (Direct Memory Access) is used for timing and this is not so accurate because lots of samples are being transferred at once. Some users have reported success using DMA Block transfer but Sample Position is much preferred. If you have to use DMA Block, the audio buffers must be set correctly so use the Detect Buffer Size and Check Buffers and Sync option in the window.

   Unfortunately, some sound cards do not support Sample Position. If yours is one and you experience timing problems, check the suggestions in the Troubleshooting section of this book but if they don't work you may want to consider buying a card which does support Sample Position.

Figure 1.4 Use Sample Position for MIDI and audio synchronisation if you can

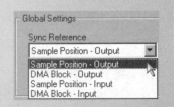

Set the Card Options

In the Card Options drop-down menu in the Global Settings section of the ASIO Multimedia Setup Advanced Options page (read it slowly!), Figure 1.5, there are three options which ought to be set correctly to get the best from your sound card.

Figure 1.5 The Card Options help with Full Duplex recording

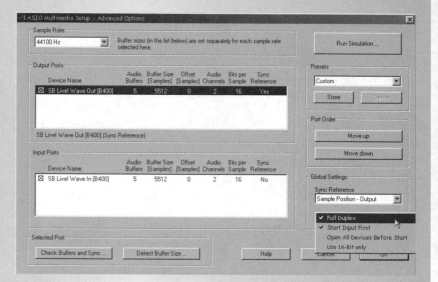

If you want to record and playback at the same time, check the Full Duplex option.

If full duplex doesn't seem to work but your card supports it, check the Start Input First option. This starts the card's input before its output which may fix things.

The Open All Devices Before Start is for use with multiple I/O cards. If you have one, this should be checked. If the card doesn't seem to be working as it should, deselect it.

PC processors

Cubase VST on the PC was designed to work with a genuine Intel processor. Although it will run with processors by other manufacturers, such as Cyrix and AMD, note that it is not guaranteed to do so.

Quite how other processors might affect performance is a bit of a grey area although most of the concern about the importance of using an Intel Pentium lies in the use of the FPU (Floating Point Unit) for real-time processing. VST makes much use of the FPU, particularly for running real-time effects which makes it difficult to recommend anything other than a Pentium (although the other processors may be fine for general home and business use). VST also specifically supports the Pentium III and makes use of the chip's extra instructions to improve digital audio processing performance.

If you want to discuss the issue, contact your local Steinberg technical support department. But it's worth bearing in mind if you're looking to upgrade or buy a new PC.

How much RAM?

The specs suggest that Cubase VST ought to run with 32Mb or even 24Mb RAM. And it usually will. However, it will run more efficiently with more. The total amount of RAM it uses depends on many things, particularly the number of Tracks (which you set in the Audio System Setup dialog), the sample rate, and how many real-time effects you have running.

If you run short of physical RAM, the program will start to use the hard disk as storage space which will, of course, slow things down. If you are working with large projects and/or using lots of real-time effects, then 128Mb RAM is not an unreasonable amount for optimum performance, and you really ought to consider 64Mb as a minimum.

If you're running a Mac with lots of memory, increase VST's memory allocation. Close VST, highlight the VST icon and select Get Info from the File menu, Figure 1.6. Increase the memory requirements and close the window.

It will help if you close other applications while running Cubase.

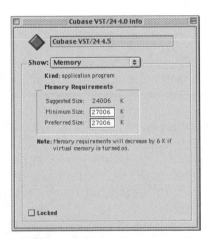

Figure 1.6 Increasing VST's memory allocation on the Mac will improve performance

Hard drives

If you're using VST for direct-to-disk recording, the choice of hard drive and its maintenance are as important as your choice of computer.

SCSI vs. EIDE drives
For optimum performance, users are traditionally recommended to use a SCSI drive and, indeed, that is Steinberg's recommendation. But it's not essential. A standard EIDE drive will still give a reasonable performance although a fast UltraDMA EIDE is very much preferred.

The benefit of SCSI is that it supports faster drives, several drives can be used on the one SCSI bus, additional drives can easily be added, and data transfer is smoother. IDE drives do not support simultaneous access which means you cannot read data from two separate drives at the same time. The drives can switch pretty quickly but data transfer will not be as quick as it would be using SCSI drives. The difference may not be enormous but it could be crucial if you want to get the most out of your system.

Some users opt for a primary EIDE drive plus a SCSI drive dedicated to digital audio. This seems like a good compromise but the system cannot read from the EIDE and the SCSI drive simultaneously so to fully optimise your system, use SCSI drives all round.

AV drives
Other advice given to digital audio users often involves plumping for an AV drive although trying to get precise information out of a supplier as to whether or not a drive really is AV, is not always easy. Quite frankly, many of them don't know and you may have to ask the manufacturer directly.

However, recent developments in drive technology have rendered this of much less importance than it once was. Without getting too technical (and there's lots of technical info on the Web if you really want to know), early drives used a method of positioning the heads above the disk platters which could require this time-out thermal recalibration. Modern drives, however, position the heads more accurately removing the need for thermal recalibration. So, this ought not to be a problem with modern drives. You may still see some drives designated as AV and this is generally to confirm their suitability for AV use – either that or they're rather old...

AV – don't worry about it.

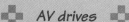

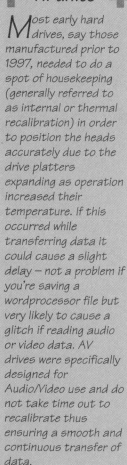

AV drives

Most early hard drives, say those manufactured prior to 1997, needed to do a spot of housekeeping (generally referred to as internal or thermal recalibration) in order to position the heads accurately due to the drive platters expanding as operation increased their temperature. If this occurred while transferring data it could cause a slight delay – not a problem if you're saving a wordprocessor file but very likely to cause a glitch if reading audio or video data. AV drives were specifically designed for Audio/Video use and do not take time out to recalibrate thus ensuring a smooth and continuous transfer of data.

Big disk

As a rule of thumb, a CD-quality (16-bit 44.1kHz) stereo digital audio recording uses around 10Mb of disk space per minute. A five-minute track would, therefore, require around 50Mb and if you're creating an eight-track, five-minute song you could be using up to 400Mb of disk space.

In practice, an eight-track recording is unlikely to use 400Mb of space because most tracks will not be filled from start to finish. But then, that doesn't take into account the out-takes, scratch files and samples you may also have stored on your hard disk during production. Grab your calculator and work out how much disk space a 16-track album would require. Now multiply by 1.5 if you're recording at 24-bit...

In other words, the message is – digital audio recording uses a lot of disk space so don't skimp on the hard drive. Get the biggest and fastest you can afford.

You also need to consider backing-up and archiving your music (see Chapter 17 for more about this).

Using two drives

It's a good idea to dedicate a hard drive to audio use. If you're doing a lot of digital audio recording, spreading the tracks onto two or more hard drives may improve performance although any benefits here are most likely to be seen with SCSI drives.

However, with a dedicated audio drive, you can use it for a project, back up the files, wipe it clean and you're ready to go with another project. It's convenience as much as performance.

Disk drive specs

If you're looking for a new hard drive, here are some specs it ought to meet or beat:

9ms average seek time (not the same as average access time)
20ms average access time (not the same as average seek time)
10Mb/sec data transfer rate
5Mb/sec sustained data transfer rate
7200rpm (54000 rpm absolute minimum)

With a comparably fast computer, suitably optimised, such a drive ought to achieve at least 8 stereo or 16 mono tracks although this obviously depends on other aspects of the system. A faster drive will manage more tracks, other aspects of the system being suitably speedy.

FireWire and USB drives

Although SCSI is likely to remain the preferred choice for digital recording for a year or two, other systems are coming on-line, FireWire in particular.

With the launch of a new range of G3 Macs in 1999, Apple forswore the SCSI interface altogether in favour of FireWire. It does, indeed, offer potentially superior performance – but few FireWire devices were actually available at the time of the launch...

Apple also helped bring the USB (Universal Serial Bus) to prominence in 1998 with the launch of the iMac which had no other ports at all! USB offers a data transfer rate of up to 12Mb/sec. While this is better than the 5Mb/sec and 10Mb/sec offered by early SCSI systems it's a far cry from the 20Mb, 40Mb and 80Mb/sec transfer rates promised by current SCSI devices. USB drives, therefore, cannot be considered for serious digital audio use.

But if you have a FireWire-compatible computer, it will be worth keeping an eye on the performance of FireWire drives as it is rumoured that they will rule the world one day.

Disk compression

Just in case it needs to be said – don't use a disk compression utility. Don't use it with digital audio, don't use it with your normal application files or with data.

You don't want to use it with digital audio files because it slows down the system. You don't want to use it full stop, not only because it slows down the system but because if there is a glitch, compressed data is much more difficult to recover.

Hard drives are relatively inexpensive so if you need more space buy another drive.

PC

You can quickly check if your PC has disk compression installed by opening the Control Panel, double-clicking on the System icon and selecting the Performance tab. The entry next to Disk Compression should say Not installed, Figure 2.1.

Figure 2.1 Check that your PC does not have disk compression installed

Fragmentation and optimisation

When you save a file to a hard disk, the system tries to save it in one continuous section. Imagine several files stored one after the other and then deleting one or two of the early ones. The process of continuously saving and then deleting files frees-up blocks on the disk which new files can be saved into. However, if a block is not large enough to hold a complete file, part of the file is saved there and part of it is saved in other free spaces. This causes files to be split or fragmented over several areas of the drive, Figure 2.2.

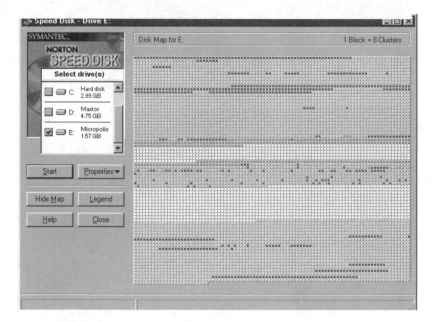

Figure 2.2 The process of saving and deleting files causes them to be split up or fragmented across the hard disk

Fragmentation slows downs the drive's ability to read the data because the drive head has to move from one area of the disk to another. And with digital audio, slow is not what we want.

The defragmentation – often called defragging – or optimisation process collects all the bits of each file and puts them in one continuous section of the disk, increasing the speed at which the files can be read, Figure 2.3.

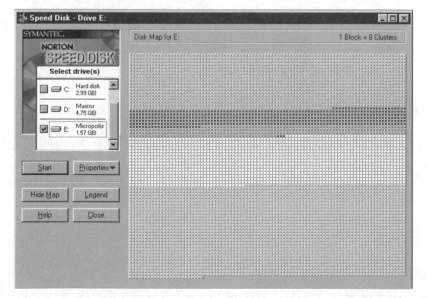

Figure 2.3 A defragged drive can read audio data much more efficiently

Do not underestimate the problems severe fragmentation can cause. You ought to defrag your hard drives before every session and again after you have saved and deleted lots of files.

Windows has a built-in in defragmentation utility which can be accessed by right-clicking on a drive in Windows Explorer, selecting Properties, clicking on the Tools tab and then on the Defragment Now button, Figure 2.4. It is, however, rather slow and Windows users might wish to consider a specialised utility such as Norton Utilities.

Figure 2.4 Windows' built-in defragmentation utility is rather slow

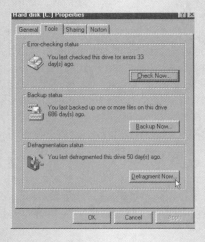

The Mac OS currently does not include a defrag function and it is essential that Mac users buy a good utility to do the job. Norton Utilities is a firm favourite and can perform many other useful checks on your disk. Just be aware that some of its background tasks can impair performance.

Working practices

Read the manuals
You *knew* this suggestion would appear in the book somewhere, didn't you? That's because it's sound advice! Okay, you hate reading manuals, but they are the best source of information about the program.

Here's a worse suggestion – read them twice! Ever read a bit in a manual which only made half-sense? The more you learn about VST, the more the other bits will fall into place. The manuals themselves are full of tips and tricks although they're not presented in that way but as operational procedures.

If you read the manuals when you got the program, read them again. You can skim through the bits you're familiar with but you will undoubtedly get more out of them the second time through.

Read the Readme file
Most versions of VST come with a Readme or a Late Changes file detailing new developments to the program, bug fixes, known bugs, tips and so on which were too late to make it into the manual. Check it out. It may contain information to assist with VST's installation, news about drivers for your sound card or new features which were added at the last minute.

Use Acrobat's Find facility
Steinberg seems to be following the rest of the herd by supplying most manuals in Adobe Acrobat format (although some versions of VST do include some printed documentation). That's probably one reason why so few people read them!

Create your own Autoload defaults file
You probably know that when VST boots it automatically loads a default file. On the PC it's called def.all, Figure 3.1, and the Mac it's called Autoload, Figure 3.2. You can tell because the filename appears in the Arrange window's header.

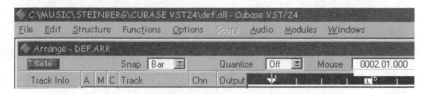

Figure 3.1 Whenever you start VST on the PC it loads the def.all file

Figure 3.2 VST on the Mac
automatically loads the
Autoload file

This file stores information such as the size and position of the windows, the Preferences settings, Key Commands, Track names, Transport Bar settings, Mixer Maps, Grooves, MIDI Filter settings and so on.

Create your own default settings and save then as def.all or Autoload to save time whenever you start a new project. You can also create customised settings for different types of project – say one for GM, one for audio only and so on – and save them as songs. If you do this, remember to rename them as soon as you have loaded them otherwise changes will overwrite the original files. This is not so much of a worry with the def.all and Autoload files because if you try to save them the program prompts for a filename.

However, some versions of VST can save a file as a Stationery document. This is essentially like a normal Song save but it cannot be saved using the 'Save' option; you must use 'Save as', Figure 3.3.

Figure 3.3 Saving a file as a
stationery document
prevents you from
accidentally overwriting it

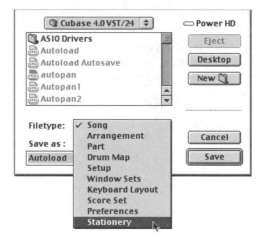

You can use this to create and save several different template files, safe in the knowledge that you cannot accidentally overwrite them. You might like to save the Autoload file in this format, too.

Naming of the ports
You can change the default names of the MME Ins and Outs using the MME Setup program, Figure 3.4. Change the names of the ports to those of the attached instruments. This is particularly useful if you have more than one MIDI Out. You can also change the names of the ports in the Advanced Option of the ASIO Multimedia Setup window by double-clicking on the port names.

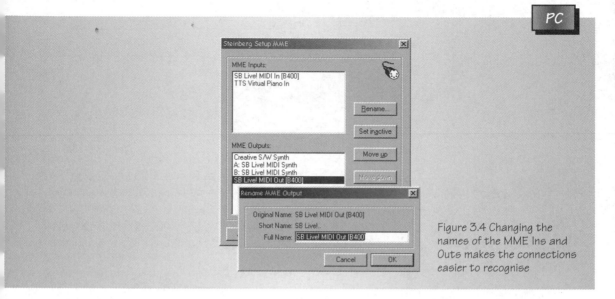

Figure 3.4 Changing the names of the MME Ins and Outs makes the connections easier to recognise

Save with song

The are several occurrences of the 'Save with song' check box in VST – in the Audio System Setup dialog, Figure 3.5, and in the Preferences General dialog box, Figure 3.6, for example. When it is checked, you have to save the Song in order to keep the settings you have made. If the box is not checked, the settings you make will be saved in VST's Preferences when you quit.

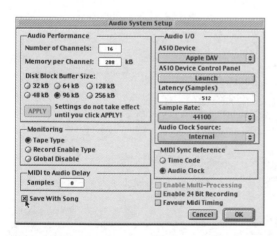

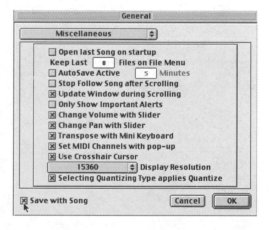

Use this check box when creating the Autoload song described above. It's particularly useful for creating your preferred audio settings such as the number of audio channels.

Figure 3.5 and Figure 3.6 Save with song appears in several VST dialogs

Thru and Thru

The Thru function, selected from the Options>MIDI Setup menu, Figure 3.7, is particularly useful when using a multi-timbral keyboard for recording, and whose sounds you also want to use for playback.

Figure 3.7 It's generally useful to enable MIDI thru

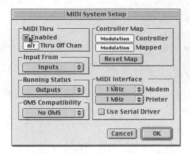

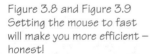
When Thru is enabled it transmits incoming MIDI data back through the MIDI Out socket. VST transmits this information on the MIDI channel of the currently-selected Track. So, for example, you can set each Track to a different MIDI channel – Track 1 to channel 1, Track 2 to channel 2 and so on, like the default setup – and assign each Track a sound in the Inspector.

If you are using one keyboard to record and playback, put it into multi-timbral mode and switch Local Control off. Now to hear any of the sounds, all you do is select the relevant Track in VST. Whatever you play will be echoed through the computer's MIDI Out on the MIDI channel of the selected Track and the relevant sound in the keyboard will play.

Thru Off Channel

If your keyboard does not have a Local Control function (they're normally hidden in a Utility menu somewhere), use the Thru Off Chan function. This lets you select a MIDI channel which will not be echoed through the Out socket. Normally, you'd set it to the MIDI channel the keyboard is transmitting on.

Speedy Gonzales

Open the Mouse Control Panel and set it to its highest speed, Figure 3.8. Some mice have special drivers and Control Panels, Figure 3.9, where you can adjust more esoteric settings such as acceleration, orientation, pointer visibility and so on.

Figure 3.8 and Figure 3.9 Setting the mouse to fast will make you more efficient – honest!

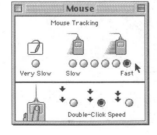

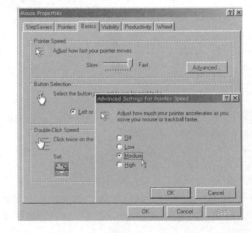

If you have been using a low mouse speed, the faster speed may seem strange at first but you'll soon get used to it. You won't have to move the mouse so far to access the whole screen area which makes operation quicker and your wrist won't be working so hard so it's less likely to tire.

Windows Sets

Windows Sets are among the best features introduced in version 4. They allow you to tailor the screen layout, including window appearances and settings and save them, enabling you to switch between several work top views very quickly. You could flick between a dedicated mixer view, for example, and the Arrange page. Windows Sets are stored in the main Preferences file and so are used with all Songs.

Figure 3.10 Windows Sets are great for switching quickly between desktop views

To create a Windows Set, simply set up the screen as you want it and select Windows>Windows Sets>New Window Set, Figure 3.10. Sets you have previously defined appear at the bottom of this menu for quick selection. To make selection even quicker, you could also set up Key Commands to switch between Windows Sets.

Track Views

VST v4 also introduced additional and selectable Track columns. Click and hold on a Track column header such as Track, Chn, Instrument and so on, and a list of the available columns pops up, Figure 3.11. Selecting all of these and viewing them all would leave no room on the screen for the arrangement, which is why they are selectable.

Figure 3.11 You can use the Track columns feature to customise the Track column layout

However, different situations may demand different combinations of columns. When recording, for example, you might want the Track, Chn and Output columns. When arranging you might want to see settings such as Volume, Pan, Velocity, Transpose, GM Name and so on.

Enter Track Views. These let you store and recall Track column selections. To store a setting, hold down the Option key while clicking on a Track header, Figure 3.12. Previously-stored Views are listed at the bottom of this menu.

Figure 3.12 Track Views make
it easy to switch to different
Track Column layouts

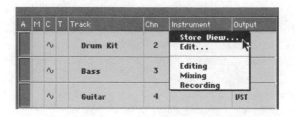

Use Key Commands

Yes, Key Commands are the tools of the real Power User. You've probably seen them – hands dancing over the computer keyboard scarcely
touching the mouse, while the screen flicks from function to function as if
under automatic control.

At the very least you should learn the Key Commands for controlling
the Transport functions. Here are the main ones which are on the numeric keypad:

Numeric keypad Key Commands

*	record		
Enter	play/continue		
0 or spacebar	1st press: stop	2nd press: go to Left Locator	3rd press: go to position 1.1.0
1	Go to Left Locator		
2	Go to Right Locator		

There's a list of Key Commands in the Appendix (page 134). Try learning
one or two new commands each session.

Shift work

You can scroll up and down through parameter values on the PC with the
right and left mouse buttons. Holding down Shift while you do so changes
the value in increments of 10. Use this with a transpose parameter and it
changes in increments of 12 – an octave.

This also works on the Mac although you need to position the cursor
carefully, a little above or below the parameter, according to which way
you want it to go when you click. VST version 4 introduced sliders, mini-
keyboards and pop-up menus which has made adjusting parameters much
easier and made many scrolling parameters redundant.

Toolbar tonic

Of course, there are those who simply cannot learn the myriad of
keystrokes required to become a power user. For you – the Toolbar,
Figure 3.13, introduced in VST version 4. Quite simply, it's a long bar into
which you can enter lots of icons which activate your most frequently
required functions. It floats, so you can place the Toolbar at a convenient
position on the screen and when you move the cursor over an icon, the
name of the function it actives appears beneath it.

Figure 3.13 The Toolbar –
Key commands for the rest
of us

The Toolbar is opened from the Windows menu. To add items to it, use the Preferences>Key Commands>Edit menu and simply click in the Icon column to add the command to the Toolbar, Figure 3.14.

Figure 3.14 You can easily customise the Toolbar so it contains your most commonly used functions

Tools for the job

The Tools have always been one of Cubase's strengths, enabling you to perform a number of functions very quickly – moving, cutting, pasting, deleting and so on. You must be familiar with the main Tools – otherwise you wouldn't be able to do diddly squat with the program – but with the release of version 4, several new Tools were added. The Tools sometimes have slightly different functions, depending on which editor you are in. There's a summary in the Appendix (page 146).

Toolbox tips

There are two useful options in the Preferences>General>Arrangement dialog, Figure 3.15. If you check the Allow Tools on Track List box, it enables the use of the Pencil and Eraser to add and delete Tracks in the area to the left of the Arrange page. It also allows the use of the Glue Tube, Logical and Groove Tools so you can and apply grooves to an entire Track, for example.

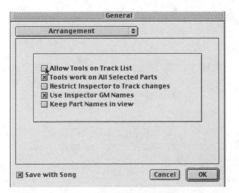

Figure 3.15 This check box lets you use Tools in the Track List

However, if you use this option be very careful about what Tool is selected when you move the cursor to the Track List. Most changes to the Track parameters require the use of the Arrow Tool and if the Pencil or Eraser is selected you could find yourself adding or deleting Tracks accidentally. For general editing it's probably best to leave this option unchecked and check it only if you want to perform functions specifically in the Track List.

The 'Tools work on All Selected Parts' option enables Tool operations to work across all selected parts – obvious, really – rather than just the one you click on. In most cases you will want to check this box.

MAC

You can open the Toolbox by holding down the Control key and clicking the mouse. The Toolbox will open under the cursor.

You can also 'tear off' the Toolbox from the menu and drag it to a new place on the screen.

Turn file sharing/networking off
Just in case you are linked to another computer, if you are having performance problems, switch this off as networking can impair performance.

Fast copying
Here's a quick way to copy parts. Select the Pencil Tool and hold down the Alt key on the PC or the Option key on the Mac. Put the Pencil on the Part you want to copy and click and drag it to the right. This will create multiple copies of the part.

Fast Ghost parts
On the PC, select the Pencil Tool, hold down Ctrl and drag as if copying a Part as above. This creates Ghost parts instead of real parts which you can identify by their name which will be in italics.

On the Mac, use the Pencil Tool and hold down both the Option and Command keys.

You can also create Ghost parts one at a time with the Pointer while holding down the Command key on the Mac and the Control key on the PC.

Fast Quantize and Snap values
Press the numeric keys at the top of the computer's keyboard to select Quantize and Snap values in any editor. Press T to toggle triplets on and off. This also works in the Arrange page but it only selects the Quantize setting, not the Snap value.

Note that this does not work with the numeric keypad as that is used for location points.

Cancel it!
You've been editing a Part in one of the editors. It's quite a complex edit and everything seems to be going well – until something goes wrong. Undo can't get you out of it and you wish you were back with the original

material. No problem, simply press the Escape key and up will pop a dialog box asking if you want to cancel all the changes you've just made or keep the edits. Click on the appropriate box and be grateful that the VST programmers know we all make mistakes.

Get organised

It's a good idea to keep all the parts and files associated with a song in their own folder. When you start a new song, save it immediately in its own folder and when you record the audio parts, save them in the folder, too. This makes it far easier to keep track of files than if they are scattered all over a disk or two.

Making notes

Did you know that Cubase has a Notepad? You'll find it lurking near the bottom of the Edit menu. Few people know it's there; even fewer people use it. It's very useful for making notes about the song: which sounds were used (if you don't save them along with the song – see next tip), what outboard effects units were used, and their settings, how the equipment was connect – anything, in fact which might help you if you come to do a remix in six months time. You may think you'll remember it all – but you won't...

Save synth settings with the song

VST can record and save SysEx data. If yours can't, make sure that the SysEx Record filter is not switched on in the MIDI Filter dialog, Figure 3.16, accessed from the Options menu.

Figure 3.16 If you want to record SysEx data, make sure the Sysex filter is not on

Use this facility to record the sounds and settings in your synths and save them to disk in the same folder as the other song data. Most synths have a Bulk Dump facility hidden behind a menu option somewhere which will transmit this data when triggered. It ensures that all the data for a song is safely stored in the same place. By all means save synth data to floppy disks and put them in a safe place but if you write many pieces you'll find the first option is much easier.

METAPHYSICAL
INFO

*Jesus saves. Moses
invests...
Yep, we're talking
serious advice here!*

Save regularly

You must, must, must save your work regularly. You're not my granny and you can probably suck eggs as well as the next Senior Cit but remember, there are only two types of computer user:

1   Those who have lost their data
2   Those who are going to

It is very important – nay, essential – therefore, that you get into a saving routine. The easiest way is to familiarise yourself with the Save shortcut keys. On the PC they are Ctrl and S. On the Mac they are Command and S. After every recording or edit which you are happy with, press these keys and save your work.

Autosave

On the other hand, you can get VST to save for you. There is an Autosave function in the Preferences window, Figures 3.17 and 3.18, which will save your song every so-many minutes. This might seem like the answer but what happens if you have just performed a rather devastating edit which has so completely marmalised your song that you decide to load the previously-saved version but before you can, the Autosave function kicks in...? Whoops....!

*Figure 3.17 and Figure 3.18
VST can save your song
automatically every so-many
minutes*

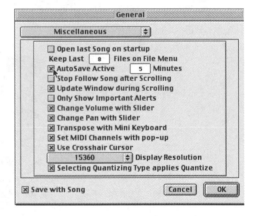

If you've a memory like a sieve, turn on Autosave, otherwise practise that Save shortcut.

You can get back to the last saved version of a song quite easily with the Revert to Saved command on the File menu. Note, however, that this only recognises a manual save, not an Autosave or a Save Backup save.

Save Backup

As you work on a song, it's a good idea to save incremental versions of it. You can use the Save As function to do this but VST has an alternative – Save Backup which you'll find on the File menu.

When you select this, the program creates a complete copy of the song using the same name but with an additional and incrementing number. So if your song was called, imaginatively, MySong the first backup would be MySong 1, the second would be MySong 2 and so on.

Program Change numbers

When you're working with MIDI you will undoubtedly need to insert Program Change numbers into the Parts to make sure they playback with the right sounds. Cubase lets you do this in two or three ways, each with their pros and cons.

An easy option is to set the sounds in the Inspector (VST v4 also includes the ability to select sounds from Track Columns). This has the advantage of being easily seen and you can change it in real-time. The possible disadvantage is that the changes are always implemented at the beginning of a Part.

Many users prefer to insert Program Changes directly into the Parts. They cannot be changed from the Arrange window and they will override the Inspector setting if the event occurs after the start of playback. However, they can easily be edited and they can be entered anywhere in a Part allowing several instrument Parts to play one after the other on one Track.

Some PC versions of VST include a GM/GS/XG editor, Figure 3.19, accessed from the Edit menu which has the benefit of showing at a glance what the 16 MIDI channels are set to. Like the Inspector, these settings are sent out at the start of the song.

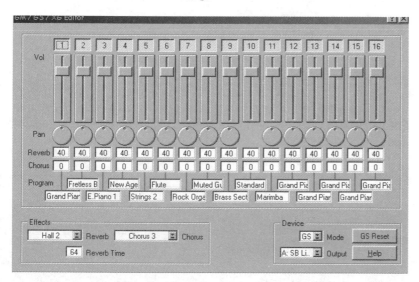

Figure 3.19 VST's GM editor which you'll find in PC versions

Program Change delays

Most MIDI devices require a short time to change to a new Program number. If you send a Program Change message followed immediately by a note, the note may not sound or it may be choked off. To avoid this, send a Program Change message a few ticks before any note data.

You may have to experiment a little to get this right as it all depends upon the synth or sound module. Some react very quickly and you may well be able to follow a Program Change message directly with a note. However, if you are creating a MIDI file to be played on unknown equipment – such as a GM module – you ought to leave some space between the two.

In VST v4 there is a Play Parameter Delay setting in the MIDI Playback Preferences window, Figure 3.20. Positive values send out the Program Change message in advance of the Part starting to play. If the value is too small (too close to 0) the notes could choke, if it's too large the instrument could change sounds before the previous Part has finished playing.

Figure 3.20 The Play Parameter Delay can help stop notes being choked by Program Change messages

Item	State/Value
Groups do play muted Parts	On
Send Real Note Off events	Off
Notes always have Priority	On
Play Parameter Delay	0. 800
Shorten notes to avoid congestion	0. 40
Chase Mixer Data	On
Chase Note Events	On
Chase Controller Events	On
Chase Program Changes	On
Chase Aftertouch	On
Chase Pitchbend	On
Chase Sysex	Off
Chase RPN/NRPN	Off

It's good and it's useful but you can be more accurate and consistent if you set up Program Changes yourself.

Finding Program Changes and other events in a Part

Sometimes your parts get so full of data that can't see the wood for the trees. If you're particularly untidy and tend to slap lots of Program Change data and other Controller data into a file it may be useful to know just exactly where it all is.

You can find this out very easily. In the upper part of the Options>Part Appearance menu, make sure that Show Events is ticked, Figure 3.21. In the lower half tick the events that you want to see.

Figure 3.21 Show Events helps identify MIDI data in tracks

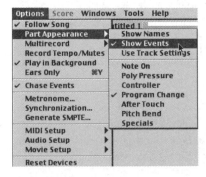

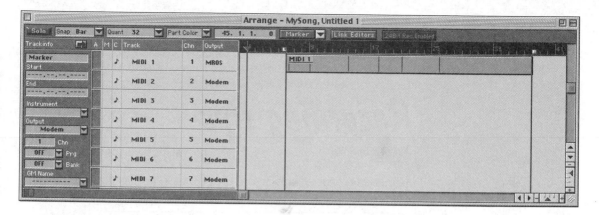

Now when you view a Part in the Arrange window the events will be indicated by lines, Figure 3.22.

Figure 3.22 With Show Events selected, MIDI data is indicated by lines

Stereo recording

Virtually all music is now created in stereo – and much of the music for movies and theatres is created in 3D – so bear this in mind when creating an arrangement. In particular, decide if the audio parts need to be in mono or stereo. A stereo sax or vocal, for example, won't sound very realistic if you pan the two channels hard left and hard right. And while it might sound cool to spread the drums in a drum set around the stereo image, again, that's not realistic. But don't let that stop you, 'cause lots of records feature drums or individual drums such as hi hats, panned hard left and right.

It often helps to create a rough stereo mix while recording so you can hear how the parts fit together.

4

Recording tips

Create a song folder

When you start a new song, it's good practice to save all the files pertaining to the song in the same folder (yes, this tip did appear in Chapter 3 but it's a good un' and bears repeating). When you're recording audio you have to specify a location where the audio files will be saved. Although the system for doing this may change in a future release, currently on the PC when you attempt to record on an audio Track a dialog box opens prompting you to select a folder for the audio. On the Mac, the audio files folder is selected from Options>Audio Setup>Audio Files Folder, Figure 4.1.

Figure 4.1 On the Mac you select a folder for the audio files from the Options menu

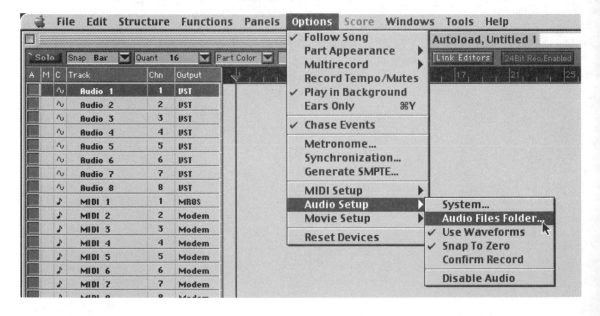

Name those audio Tracks

Before recording any audio Tracks, change the Track names to something more meaningful than Audio 1, Audio 2, etc. When VST saves an audio file to disk, it uses the Track name as the name of the file. Giving the Tracks meaningful names makes them much easier to find if you want to edit them outside VST. Also, subsequent takes are given the same name with a number suffix, again, making them easy to find.

❖ INFO ❖

There are tips on finding lost audio files in Chapter 13.

Don't share audio files

If you have audio files which you want to use with more than one song, it is highly recommended that you copy the files to each of the song folders rather than trying to share them. This will save much heartache later.

Changing audio file names

If you decide you want to change the name of an audio file after recording, change it in the Audio Pool by double-clicking on it and entering another name, Figure 4.2. This enables VST to keep track of the file.

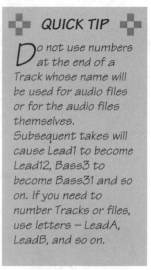

QUICK TIP

Do not use numbers at the end of a Track whose name will be used for audio files or for the audio files themselves. Subsequent takes will cause Lead1 to become Lead12, Bass3 to become Bass31 and so on. If you need to number Tracks or files, use letters – LeadA, LeadB, and so on.

File Name	Disk	S/M	Resolution	Img	Length	Date
Hear Segment		Start	End	Length	SRate	Range
▷ Track55t_ell.wav	D:	○	16 Bit	↔	3.993K	08/10/98
▷ neu_Track_58_tk6.waD:		○	16 Bit	↔	495K	08/10/98
▷ neu_Track_58_tk7.waD:		○	16 Bit	↔	1.237K	08/10/98
▷ neu_Track_58_tk8.wav		○	16 Bit	↔	4.732K	08/10/98
▷ Sinemelo_tel.wav	D:	○	16 Bit	↔	4.208K	08/10/98
▷ Sinemelo_tel.wav	D:	○	16 Bit	↔	4.084K	08/10/98
▷ Sinemelo_a0.wav	D:	○	16 Bit	↔	1.732K	08/10/98
▷ Chor Male.wav	D:	∞	16 Bit	↔	3.961K	08/10/98
▷ Chor Edith.wav	D:	∞	16 Bit	↔	3.961K	08/10/98
▷ Add Chor.wav	D:	∞	16 Bit	↔	3.961K	08/10/98

Figure 4.2 Change the name of an audio file in the Audio Pool so VST can keep track of it

If you change the file name directly on the hard disk with the Finder (Mac) or Explorer (PC), VST will not be able to find it when it loads the song again. It will, however, warn you of this when you open the song and you have the option of skipping the file, letting VST find it or finding it manually. VST is very strict about identifying files and requires that the name and date are correct. If you've messed with these you'll need to find the file manually. If these two attributes are not the same as the original file, VST will warn you of this but still let you load the file.

Selecting a suitable sample rate

What's the best sample rate to use? VST supports several sample rates although what you can use is also dependent on the capabilities of your audio hardware. Using the built-in audio capabilities of a PowerMac, for example, you will only be able to select 44.1kHz, Figure 4.3. Plug in a dedicated digital audio card and you may have more options. On the PC, a sound card might support a wide range of sample rates from 11.025kHz to 96kHz.

You will get better quality audio the higher the sample rate you use, and if you have the disk space and the processing power to work at 96kHz then go for it. However, most people manage quite well at 44.1kHz so you can be quite happy working at that. Some people try to save disk space and maybe some processing power by using 32kHz. This may be acceptable as a half-way house, say if you want to post 'reasonable' quality files on the Internet but it cannot really be recommended for music.

If you record to or backup to DAT, you might want to use 48kHz which many DAT recorders use. In fact, some cannot use 44.1kHz. The benefit of using the same rate is that the audio need not be converted while recording to and from the DAT.

Figure 4.3 Using the built-in
audio facilities of a
PowerMac you can only
select a 44.1 kHz sampling
rate

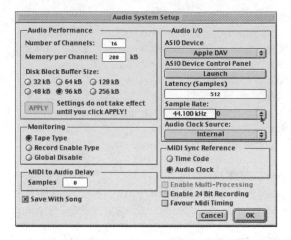

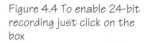 INFO

*'Divn't fash yersel''
– a colloquial
expression from our
friends in the North
East meaning 'don't
worry yourself'.*

As most recordings end up on CD at 44.1kHz, you may be happy to
stick with that. It would take a jolly good pair or ears to detect the difference in quality between 44.1 and 48. That being the case, is it better to
use 44.1kHz to record to DAT? Well, the conversion (or downsampling)
to 44.1kHz will have to be done anyway but if it's done by a mastering
house they ought to have better gear than you and should make a better
job of it. So retain every last ounce of quality and use 48kHz. But divn't
fash yersel' about using 44.1kHz.

What sample resolution?

VST supports 16-bit recording. VST/24 supports both 16-bit and 24-bit
recording. To switch it on, you simply click on the Enable 24 Bit
Recording button in the Audio>System dialog, Figure 4.4. You need a
compatible audio card to be able to use 24-bit recording, however.

Figure 4.4 To enable 24-bit
recording just click on the
box

In case you're wondering, yes 24-bit recording is noticeably higher
quality than 16-bit recording, assuming you have quality playback equipment to compare them. Virtually all professional digital audio systems
now use at least 24-bit recording.

Again, you might wonder if 24-bit is worth using as it's converted to 16-bit when it's burned to CD. And the answer, again, is yes. When converted to 16-bit, a quality 24-bit recording will be higher quality than a recording made at 16-bit throughout its production. And when CDs become 24-bit you'll already have the masters to cut a new one. Although by then we will probably have moved on to 32-bit recording...

But, again, if you only have a 16-bit system or if running at 24-bit is putting too much strain on your system, be happy with 16 bits. It's still far higher quality than tape recording...

Record everything
With version 4, VST was given the ability to record everything! It is always in Record mode so if you are listening to some tracks, doodling around and just happen to play the most brilliant riff in the world, don't worry if VST was not 'officially' recording.

All you do is to click on the Record button while holding down the Option key (on the Mac). The contents of the MIDI buffer are turned into a Part and placed on the Record Track at the current Song Position.

Don't overdrive the levels
This is for anyone who has migrated to digital audio recording from tape recording. With a tape recorder, you may be used to pushing the level, lifting the volume fader up just a little higher to get 'more sound' onto the tape. Because of the characteristics of tape, this overdriving effect is a form of compression and the resulting sound can appear bigger and warmer than recording at a 'safe' level.

You can't do this with digital recording. The characteristics of digital and analogue recording are completely different and if you try to overdrive the signal, the only thing you will add to the sound is distortion. So don't try.

Record every part at as high a level as you can without clipping. There is a range of digital audio plug-ins which can add 'warmth' and 'analogue feel' to a recording afterwards if you feel it needs it.

Recording live
Live recording is far more difficult than recording synths and electronic gear – if you've tried it you'll know! The main criteria are to keep an even volume level and to ensure that it doesn't peak into distortion.

Recording vocals
Vocals are one of the most difficult sounds of all to record. A vocalist with a little mic technique who can keep a constant volume level is a great asset. A good microphone helps, too. Use a pop shield to reduce the plosives and sibilance. If the vocals still need a little tidying up, there are De-esser plug-ins and compressors which can smooth out rough edges.

Monitoring without delay
When recording into VST, you'll probably to want to hear pre-recorded Tracks so you can play in time with them. There are a couple of ways of

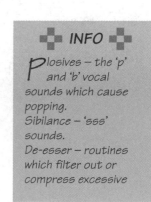

** INFO **

Plosives – the 'p' and 'b' vocal sounds which cause popping.
Sibilance – 'sss' sounds.
De-esser – routines which filter out or compress excessive

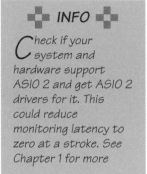

✦ **INFO** ✦

*C*heck if your system and hardware support ASIO 2 and get ASIO 2 drivers for it. This could reduce monitoring latency to zero at a stroke. See Chapter 1 for more

doing this. Your first choice would probably be to monitor the audio through VST. However, if you do this you may well notice a delay between what you play and when you hear it. That's the latency inherent in most digital audio systems although it can be minimised by using a digital audio card with a very low latency and an ASIO driver. Some of these cards can get the latency down to around 3ms (as of writing, this includes the Sonorus StudI/O) although a latency of 10, 12 or perhaps even 20ms may be acceptable in certain circumstances.

Another advantage of using a card with a low latency is that it enables you to route the sound through some VST digital effects. This may be useful for guitar players (or keyboard players emulating a guitar sound) who need to hear the processed sound because it affects they way they play the music lines.

An alternative, and possibly the more practical option for users with standard sound cards or ones without low-latency drivers, is to monitor at source. In other words you listen to the sound before it goes into VST for recording. This is the easiest and often the cheapest option although it does really require a mixer. You need to route the audio from the mixer to a set of monitor speakers and to VST's recording input. This is easy to do if the mixer has direct outputs, although if you can route the signal to an auxiliary output you can probably route that to your sound card.

You should also set the Monitoring option in VST's Audio System Setup window to Global Disable. Figure 4.5 shows the window on the PC, and Figure 4.6 shows the equivalent on the Mac.

Figure 4.5 and Figure 4.6 Setting the monitor option on the PC and Mac

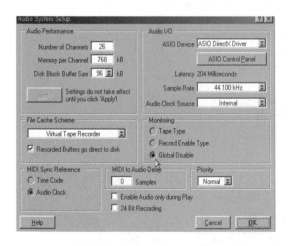
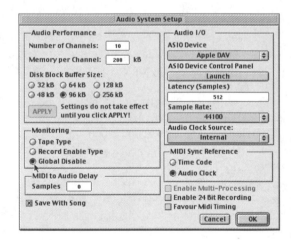

Cycle recording shortcuts

If you have difficulty remembering the shortcut keys for Cycle Record options, when you are in Cycle Record mode, click on the 'Cycle Rec' text in the Transport Bar and the options will appear in a pop-up menu, Figure 4.7. The PC version of VST is also kind enough to remind you of the shortcuts, Figure 4.8.

Figures 4.7 and 4.8 The Transport Bar can remind you of the Cycle Record shortcuts

Volume vs. Expression

When creating fades and adjusting the volume level of parts, most people probably use MIDI Volume which is Controller 7. That's what it's for after all, and VST positively encourages you to use it with the Volume parameter in the Inspector and the Volume sliders in the Track List, Figure 4.9. However, there is a case for using Controller 11, Expression, for making internal volume adjustments such as fades.

They both control volume so what's the difference? Think of Volume as the main volume control on a synth and Expression as a foot pedal which enables you to control the volume while you're playing. The main volume control sets the maximum level of the output while the pedal lets you vary the volume during playback.

Let's say you've created a fade using Volume, you come to mix the piece and discover that the part containing the fade is too loud. So you reduce its volume in the Mixer – but when the fade comes in the volume levels shoot up again. To change the entire volume of the part you have to physically reduce all the Volume data which make up the fade.

If you had used Expression to create the fade, a simple tweak with the slider would reduce the overall volume of the part, including the fade.

Figure 4.9 The Volume sliders in the Track List are not the only way of controlling volume

A	M	C	T	Track	Chn	Vol		Output
		∿		Brushes	1		-12.8	VST
		∿		Drum Kit	2		-2.4	VST
		∿		Bass	3		-1.8	VST
		∿		Guitar	4		-8.7	VST
		∿		Wah Guitar	5		-15.4	VST
		∿		Sax	6		-10.8	VST
		♪		Vibes	1		0	Modem
		♪		Strings	2		127	Modem

Solo   Snap 1/2   Quant Off   Part Color

Here's a quick way to create a fade. In the Controller editor (or, in pre-v4 versions of VST, the Controller editor below the Key editor – which v4 also has) select Expression and draw in a rough fade with the Pencil Tool, Figure 4.10. Then straighten it up with the Line Tool, Figure 4.11.

Figure 4.10 To create a quick fade, draw in the Expression data with the Pencil ...

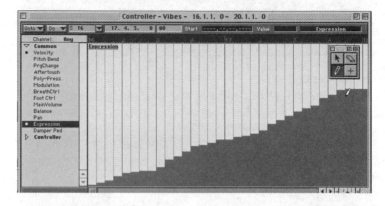

Figure 4.11 ... then straighten it with the Line Tool

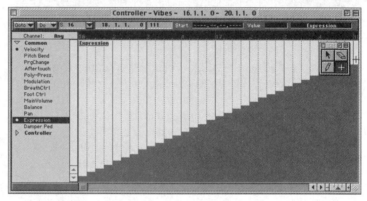

Don't tweak Velocity to adjust volume

Again, the Velocity parameter in the Inspector is a positive encouragement to use it to tinker with volume. In many cases it will work fine but it is used to control other parameters of a sound, not just volume, and this could throw you a googly if you're not careful.

Many sounds use velocity to control parameters other than volume. Increasing the velocity of a brass sound, for example, could open the filter to create a brighter sound. If you use velocity to reduce the volume you would also reduce the brightness.

So use Volume or Expression to control volume rather than Velocity.

Also bear in mind that some sounds on some instruments can distort if played at a full Velocity of 127 so it's a good idea to keep the highest values a bit lower. Just in case.

You often see arrangements where all the notes have a Velocity of 127 in pieces which have been recorded in step-time by beginners.

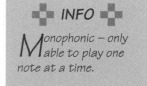

More realistic instrument sounds

To create a realistic performance of a synthesised instrument you need to play in the way an instrumentalist would play. This may seem obvious but there are a few arrangements out there containing clutches of keyboard-formed flute chords...

A key ingredient is the phrasing. Remember that wind players have to breath so note the phrasing of the line and ease off when they would be expected to take a breath.

Most solo instruments are monophonic so don't play a note before releasing the previous one. You can quickly see if you've been guilty of this in the Key editor, Figure 4.12, where 'held on' notes will overlap.

>
>
> **INFO**
>
> *M*onophonic – only able to play one note at a time.

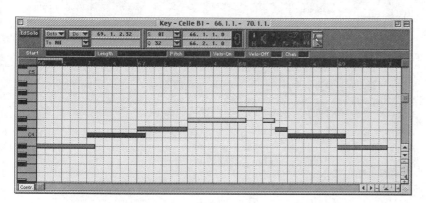

Figure 4.12 The Key editor will show if any of the notes in a 'monophonic' part overlap

Fortunately, VST has a quick solution for this with the Functions>MIDI Functions>Note Length>Del. Overlaps (poly) function. Select all the notes, select this function and the overlaps will be removed, Figure 4.13.

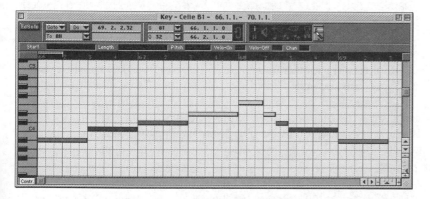

Figure 4.13 VST can remove overlaps easily

This still leaves the end of each note butting up sharply against the start of the next one which may be a bit too legato for some instruments.

But we can soon fix this with the Logical editor. Create a new preset called Reduce Length. There are only two settings to make. Set the Filter section Equal to Note. In the Processing section Keep everything except the Length and set that to Minus 0.50 (although you can alter this value to suit). In the Functions section, make sure Transform is on otherwise nothing will happen! The final preset can be seen in Figure 4.14. Select all the notes and apply the preset and the notes will shorten, Figure 4.15.

Figure 4.14 You can create a Logical function to reduce the length of notes

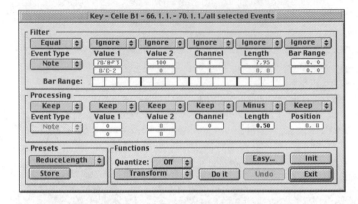

Figure 4.15 The result of shortening the notes in our monophonic part

An alternative way to record pitch bend and modulation

The most natural way to record a part which requires pitch bend or modulation widdlies is to twiddle the wheel at the same time as you play the notes. Sometimes, however, it can be difficult to hit the exact pitch you're aiming for or to get the timing right.

An alternative method is to record the part straight and then record the pitch bend or modulation later on another Track. You'll be able to hear the result of your widdles in real time and you'll be able to concentrate solely on the modulation without having to worry about the notes. And if you do it wrong it's easy to delete the Part and record it again.

Legato

You will, of course, have noticed that VST has a dedicated Legato function in the Functions>MIDI Functions>Note Length menu, Figure 4.16. This is useful if you tend to play a little staccato and need a flowing line.

Even so, and depending on the sound you are using, you may find that reducing the length of legato notes a little as described above may produce a better result.

Better than tick-tock

When you're doodling and laying down a few ideas, the metronome's tick-tock is not the most creatively-stimulating sound in the universe. You can

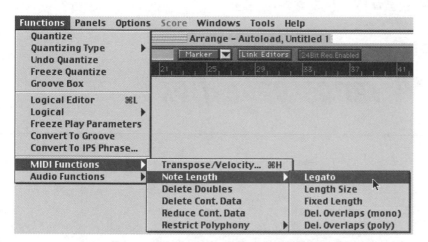

Figure 4.16 The Legato function is useful if you tend to play staccato!

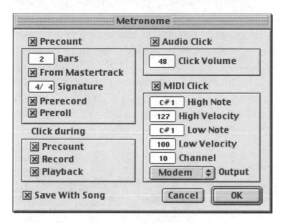

Figure 4.17 You can create a range of different ticks and tocks for the metronome to play

change the sounds used by the Metronome in the Metronome setup box, Figure 4.17, which is normally used to select drum sounds for the high and low metronome clicks.

However, instead of the tick-tock, you could create a Styletrax pattern to play along to. Alternatively, you could use a MIDI drum Track, something which grooves along in the style of the music you are creating. This could be something you created earlier for another song or an off-the-shelf song – see next item. Another alternative is to use an audio drum loop. None of these need feature in the finished work, they're simply there to help you get going. Far better than tick-tock.

A little help from our friends...

If you're struggling to find that perfect bass line or drum loop, why not let the pros give you a hand? There are dozens of MIDI files and sample CDs available, produced by top-notch musicians covering a vast range of musical styles. You'll find them advertising in the music mags and there are a few listed in the Appendix. Even if you edit these files later, they can provide backing tracks and loops to get you started – and many of them are easily good enough to find a permanent home in your recordings.

At times, we all need a little help from our friends...

5

Arrange page tips

Make a marker Track

If your arrangements have many parts which overlap each other, it's not always easy to see where one section starts and another one ends. Select a Track – the very top Track in the Arrange page is good – and make it a MIDI Track by clicking on the C column and selecting MIDI Track from the pop-up menu. Call it Marker. Insert empty parts the length of each of the sections in your song, effectively mapping out the structure of the piece. You might have a 4-bar intro, an 8-bar riff, a 16-bar chorus and so on. Name them and colour them if you wish using the Part Colors (Steinberg hasn't quite Anglicised this yet...) drop down menu at the top of the Arrange window, Figure 5.1.

Figure 5.1 It's often helpful to mark out an arrangement with blank parts

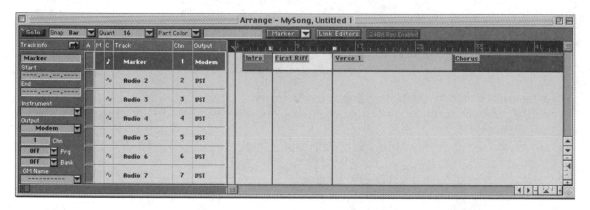

This provides a pattern for your song but it has another useful function, too. In order to hear a section, all you have to do is highlight the relevant Part and on the PC press the Alt Gr key (or Alt and Ctrl) and P (on the Mac press Option and P) and the Locators will jump to the start and end of the part. Press 1 on the Numeric Keypad and the Position Pointer will jump to the Left Locator. You can now play the section.

Marker Tracks for complex arrangements

If you have a very long or complex arrangement, you can simplify the selection of the sections by using Groups. Select each of the Marker parts (created as described above) in turn and select Build Group from the Structure menu (or use Control U on the PC) (Command U on the Mac).

Give it the same name as the Marker part. The parts will be listed down the right of the Arrange window.

Now, select a Part in the list, press the Alt Gr + P or Option + P keys as described above and then 1 on the Numeric Keypad and you're ready to play the section, Figure 5.2.

Figure 5.2 Grouped parts can be used as a quick way of playing a section of an arrangement

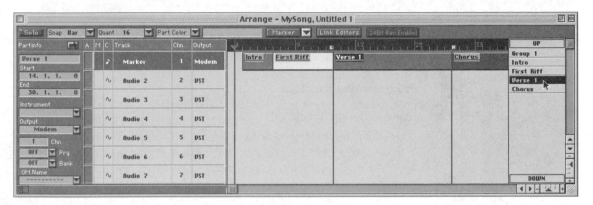

The Mac's special Marker Track

If you're wondering why these tips are included when your version of VST already has a special Marker Track, Figure 5.3, it's because earlier versions of VST did not...

Figure 5.3 Some versions of VST have a dedicated marker track

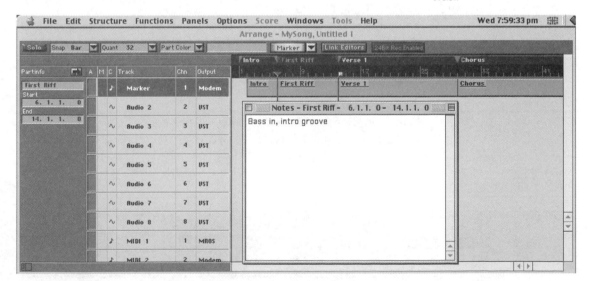

Colour my Parts

Colour can be used very effectively to help distinguish one Part from another. Even if you do no more than give each Track its own colour, this can help distinguish Tracks in the middle of a busy arrangement.

If you put different instruments on the same Track, however, then colour can be particularly effective at helping you differentiate between them.

Figure 5.4 Colour can be used to identify Parts and instruments

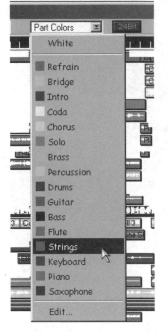

To colour a part, simply select the Part and then pick a colour from the Part Colors drop down menu. To make all the parts on a Track the same colour, highlight the Track and from the Edit menu select Select>Parts On Track and then pick the colour.

If you want to be really organised, you can name the colours according to the music sections or instruments they represent, Figure 5.4. At the bottom of the Part Color menu is an Edit option. The format differs slightly between PC and Mac but in both cases you can change the names of the colours and add new colours to the list.

Programming Locators

Locators are very useful for isolating and homing in on a section of music but it's very time-consuming to have to manually drag them to new positions when you're skipping around a song.

Fortunately, you can program the Locator positions into the Function keys. Set the Locators to their required positions and on the PC hold down Shift and press one of the Function keys from F2 to F11. To recall the Locator positions, just press the Function key.

On the Mac, hold down Option and Command and press one of the keys, 1 to 0 on the QWERTY part of the Mac's keyboard, not the Numeric keypad. To recall the positions, hold down Command and press the relevant key.

Programming Cue Points

You can also use Cue Points to locate to various positions throughout a song. To set up a Cue Point, set the Song Position to where you want the Cue Point to be, hold down Shift and press one of the keys 3 to 8 on the Numeric Keypad. To recall the Cue Point, press the relevant Keypad key.

Go to Locators

The 1 and 2 keys on the Numeric Keypad move the Song Position Pointer to the Left and Right Locators respectively. You can also send the Song Position to these points by clicking on the 'Left Locator' and Right Locator' labels (the text itself, not the numeric values) on the Transport Bar, Figure 5.5.

Figure 5.5 A click on the Locator text can move the Song Position Pointer

Quick Parts

You can create a new Part in an arrangement very quickly by double-clicking with the Pointer between the Locators.

Splitting MIDI channel data

If you have a MIDI file in Format 0 (most Format 0 files are created with hardware sequencers in mind) which you want to edit, it's often easier to do so by splitting each MIDI channel onto its own Track. VST v4 has an Explode by Channel function in its Structure menu while earlier versions have the Remix function.

The function works on the selected Track and on the area between the Locators. If possible, Parts are put on existing Tracks set to the same MIDI channel otherwise new Tracks are created.

Splitting audio Tracks

The above functions also work with audio Tracks. If an audio Track is set to Any, the events will be split onto separate Tracks according to the channel they play back on.

Splitting drum Parts into individual drums

With drum Tracks, the Explode by Channel and Remix functions (see above) split each drum note onto its own Track. This is particularly useful when creating customised or complex drum parts.

Playing multi-channel Parts

If you have a Part containing MIDI events on more than one MIDI channel, simply set the Chan setting in the Inspector to Any and each event will play on its respective MIDI channel.

Less edits with Ghost Parts

VST supports Ghost Parts. These are copies of an existing Part which 'borrow' the data in the original Part. A Ghost Part can be modified by Inspector settings, playback on a different MIDI channel, transposed and so on. However, if you edit either the original or a Ghost Part, all the Parts are changed.

Ghost Parts are ideal for any piece which uses riffs or has sequences which repeat. You only have to record the riff once and then use Ghost Parts wherever else it's required in the piece. It scores over making physical copies of a Part if you should want to change the riff – you simply change it in one Part and all the others change, too. It means there's less editing to do and you don't have to remember where all the riffs are.

To create a Ghost Part you simply hold down the Control key on the PC (the Command key on the Mac) and drag the Part you want to copy to a new location. The Ghost Part name will be in italics.

Using Groups – or not

You might expect some lyrical waxing about the power of Groups... Yes, it's powerful but it can also be confusing and the main benefit is realised with very complex arrangements which Grouping helps organise into smaller, er, groups.

The consensus of opinion is not to use Groups for the sake of it. If you find an arrangement is becoming unwieldy then look up Groups in the Getting Into The Details manual.

If you are well organised, however, you can make good use of Group Tracks. You make a Track into a Group Track by clicking in a Track's C

INFO

MIDI File Formats

There are two MIDI File Formats in common use – O and 1. In Format O files, all the data for all the MIDI channels is stored on one Track. In Format 1 files, each MIDI channel has its own Track. Format 1 files are easier to edit. Format O files are slightly smaller and often run more efficiently although neither of these factors should be a problem or worthy of consideration with the current crop of sequencers – both hard and soft. Some hardware sequencers, particularly those built into keyboards which read and play data directly from floppy disk, can only read Format O files although the more enlightened and modern keyboards support both formats.

Figure 5.6 You can make a
Track a Group Track by
selecting the option in the C
column

A	M	C	Track	Chn	Output	T	Instr
		∿	Audio 1	1	VST		
		∿	Audio 2	2	VST		
		∿	Audio 3	3	VST		
		∿	Audio 4	4	VST		
		∿	Audio 5	5	VST		
		∿	Audio 6	6	VST		
		∿	Audio 7	7	VST		
				8	VST		

∿ Audio Track
♪ MIDI Track
＼ Drum Track
◻ Folder Track
↸ Mixer Track
≋ Group Track
⌘ Tape Track
▥ Style Track
C⁷ Chord Track

				1	Modem		
				2	Modem		
				3	Modem		
				4	Modem		
				5	Modem		
				6	Modem		
		♪	MIDI 7	7	Modem		
		♪	MIDI 8	8	Modem		
		♪	MIDI 9	9	Modem		
		♪	MIDI 10	10	Modem		
		♪	MIDI 11	11	Modem		
		♪	MIDI 12	12	Modem		
		♪	MIDI 13	13	Modem		

(for Class) column and selecting Group Track from the pop-up menu,
Figure 5.6. You can then drag Groups from the Groups list (you may have
to select Show Groups from the Structure menu first) to the Track and
build up an arrangement this way.

Tempo tricks

Cubase VST has two tempo editors – the Graphical Mastertrack, Figure 6.1 and the List Mastertrack, Figure 6.2. The List is ideal for fine-tuning tempo values and positions. The Graphical editor is ideal for drawing in tempo changes and is more intuitive than the List Mastertrack.

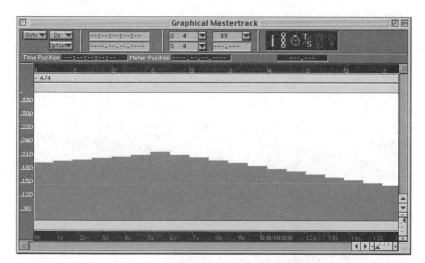

Figure 6.1 The Graphical editor provides a useful visual indication of tempo changes

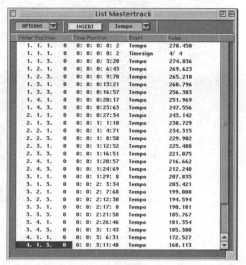

Figure 6.2 The List editor is ideal for fine tuning tempo settings

Figure 6.3 The Master
button is at the bottom
right of the Transport Bar

Master track

When the Master button in the Transport Bar is on, Figure 6.3, the tempo is controlled by the tempo events in the tempo Mastertrack. When it is off, the tempo is solely governed by the tempo setting in the Transport Bar.

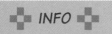

If you think it may be necessary to change the tempo after a recording has been made, try to leave the recording of any audio parts until after the changes have been finalised. Although VST includes functions for changing the tempo of audio parts, it's far easier if you don't have to do this.

Conversely, if you are using sample loops, it's usually easier to lay down the basic tracks with the loops and add MIDI parts afterwards.

This can be very useful if you need to add additional material to a recording which contains lots of tempo changes. It's far easier to record to a steady tempo than it is to follow tempo changes so simply switch off the Mastertrack, record the new parts and switch it on again.

Creating accelerandi and ritardandi

This is easy. Open the Graphical Mastertrack and resize the window to show the range of bars over which you want the change to occur. If there is already tempo data in the editor you can simply drag a line from the start tempo to the end tempo and the tempo events will change accordingly, Figure 6.4.

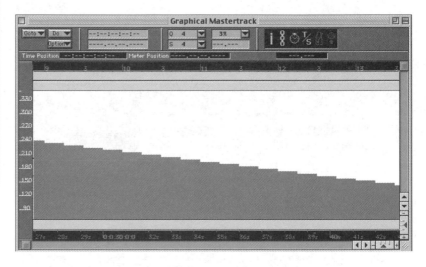

Figure 6.4 You can quickly
create tempo changes by
clicking and dragging with the
Line tool

If there are no tempo events you can draw them in with the Line by holding down Option on the Mac or Alt on the PC as you drag. The number of events entered is determined by the Snap value or the Quantize value, depending on which version of VST you have. Start with a value of 2. This ought to suffice for most tempo changes but you can increase the number of tempo events if you feel this doesn't capture the full nuances of the changes you require.

Real-time tempo recording

If you're more of a real-time, hands-on person, you can record tempo changes into VST in real-time. Check the Record Tempo/Mutes entry in the Options menu. When VST is in Record mode, this setting enables the recording of any tempo changes you make and puts them in the Mastertrack. Make sure you don't overwrite any other recording while doing this by selecting an empty Track. To enter tempo data, simply change the tempo setting in the Transport Bar.

Be aware that the Mastertrack is always in Replace mode and any tempo changes you record will replace existing tempo data. You can use the Locators and Punch In and Punch Out facilities, too, in exactly the same way as you punch in and out of a MIDI recording.

Why would you want to do this? Well, you can make tempo changes as you listen to and watch the arrangement playback which is often more intuitive than entering changes in the editor.

Remember to activate the Mastertrack in the Transport Bar for the changes to take effect.

Smoothing tempo changes

Sometimes a tempo change which you've drawn in may occur too abruptly, Figure 6.5. Fortunately, VST has a Smooth feature in the Graphical Mastertrack's Do menu which rounds off the corners, Figure 6.6.

Figure 6.5 This curve would produce an abrupt tempo change

Figure 6.6 Smoothing the curve creates a, er, smoother tempo change

Reducing tempo events

Just above the Smooth function in the Do menu, is a Reduce function which thins out tempo data. It works on selected tempo events.

This is very useful if, as a result of tempo recording, there is a particularly thick cluster of tempo data in the Mastertrack. It can slow down screen redraws as well as making it more difficult to edit the tempo events. You may be surprised by just how much you can thin out tempo data without making a noticeable difference to the playback, although in these days of fast computers and large hard disks, there's little point in thinning out the data just for the sake of it.

Tempo mapping Tracks with Timelock or creating a readable score from a rubato recording

A common problem many composers face with sequencing programs is trying to record a piece out of time, rubato, but still view it in time with all the notes positioned on their relevant beats in an editor. This is particularly problematical if you need to convert a rubato recording into a printable score.

VST offers a solution with Timelocked Tracks. A Track can be Timelocked by clicking in its T column which causes a small padlock to appear, Figure 6.7. You may have to drag the divider between the Track List and the Part display area to the right to reveal the T column or select it from the Track List menu in version 4, Figure 6.8.

Figure 6.7 You can Timelock a Track by clicking on its T column

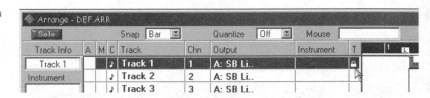

Figure 6.8 In V4 you can keep the Timelock column hidden until needed

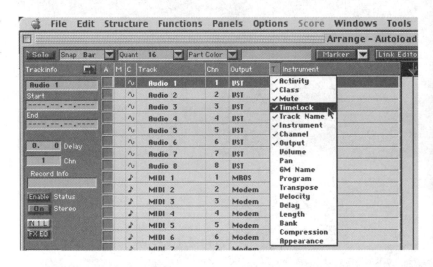

Timelocked Tracks are fixed in time so if you change the tempo, the events on the Track still stay at their same position. A note which plays five seconds into a Track will still play five seconds into the Track even if the tempo is doubled.

This has several uses such as matching music to sound effects or movie events which occur at specific time positions rather than bar and beat positions. It can also be used to fade one tempo into another – this happens in film where a scene with music at one tempo fades or crossfades into a scene with music at another tempo.

Here, however, we will look at the problem of creating a tempo map for a rubato recording so it looks correct in an editor – including the score editor – but still plays with a rubato feel. Essentially we do this by inserting tempo events into the Mastertrack so that the piece plays with a rubato feel but looks neat with the notes on the beat in an editor.

We'll use a simple example but the principle can be applied to more complex recordings. The example is a four-bar bass line recorded out of tempo. To make a rubato recording, simply switch off the metronome and record. You can see in Figure 6.9 that none of the notes is on the beat and the timing is not consistent.

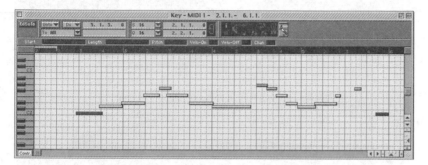

Figure 6.9 A bass line recorded out of tempo

Switch off the Master button in the Transport Bar and Timelock the Track (click the padlock on in the T column). Select all the notes and drag the first one to a suitable timing position which will usually be to the start of a bar (assuming the first note starts on the first beat of a bar), Figure 6.10.

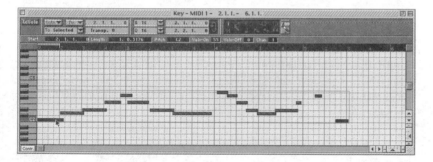

Figure 6.10 Grab the recording so the first note is on the first beat of the bar

Now select those notes which ought to fall on specific divisions of the bar. In this example, there are four notes which should fall on the first beat of each bar, Figure 6.11, but you may want to select notes which fall on the first and third beats, for example, depending on how complex the timing is. Copy the notes to the clipboard (select Copy from the Edit menu or use the shortcut keys).

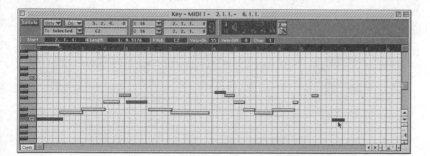

Figure 6.11 These four notes should fall exactly on the first beat of the bar

Set the Left Locator and Song Position to the start of the piece and the Right Locator to the end. Now open the Graphical Mastertrack editor and select Paste from the Edit menu. This inserts the MIDI data into the editor, Figure 6.12.

Figure 6.12 The MIDI data have been inserted into the Graphical editor at the bottom of the display

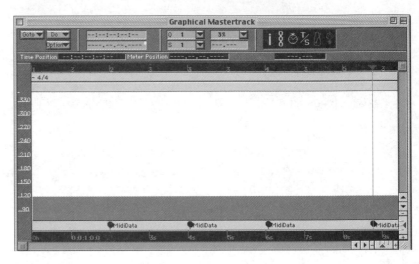

Set a Quantize value in the Graphical Mastertrack according to the bar division used in the note selection process. For example, if you selected notes on the first and third beats, then select 2. If, as in this case, only the first beats of the bars have been used, set a value of 1.

Select Fill Meter Hits from the Do menu, Figure 6.13, then select Link One by One from the Do menu, Figure 6.14. The MIDI data and Hitpoints will be linked so the next step is to straighten up the links by selecting Straighten Up from the Do menu, Figure 6.15. You can now see how the tempo is being changed from bar to bar.

Figure 6.13 Hitpoints appear at the top of the screen at exact beat positions

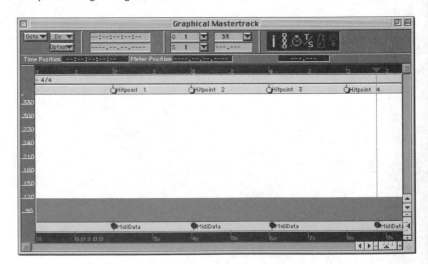

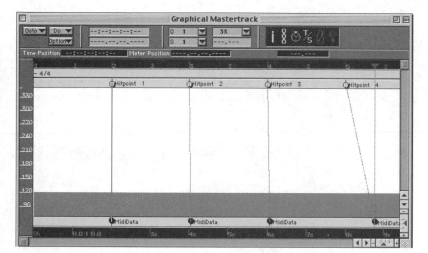

Figure 6.14 Link one by one links the Hitpoints and MIDI data

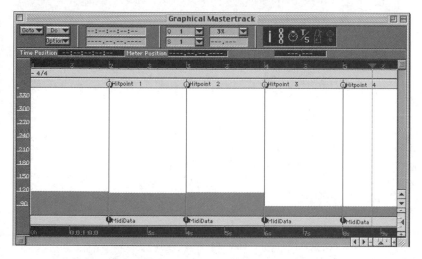

Figure 6.15 After straightening up the links, new tempo changes appear

Close the Graphical Mastertrack, switch on the Master button in the Transport and hit play.

This feature can also be used to create a printable score from a pre-recorded free style performance. In this case, what you need to do is to create another Track and either insert or play MIDI events at required tempo points, say on every beat, half beat or quarter beat. You should be able to do this by tapping along with the music. It should not be necessary to use a timing resolution shorter than quarter notes.

You would then select these notes, copy them, select a suitable Snap value, and follow the procedure outlined above.

Multiple tempo changes
You can use Timelocked Tracks to create arrangements with more than one tempo. Weird uh? This is particularly useful with visual work where hits or sound effects have to occur at specific time positions to coincide with visual cues.

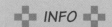

INFO

It's generally not a good idea to try to edit a Timelocked Track in an editor at the same time as you are messing with the Mastertrack editor. You could lose events.

Say you've done the music, inserted the hits and the producer decides the music would be better if it was a little faster or slower. Naturally, changing the tempo will move the cues which is not what you want.

The first step is to Timelock the Tracks which are time-sensitive, the ones containing the hits and sound effects, by clicking in the T column in the Inspector, Figure 6.16. Next, create a new tempo map for the music parts of the arrangement, the parts which have to change tempo.

Figure 6.16 Timelock those Tracks whose tempo you want to preserve

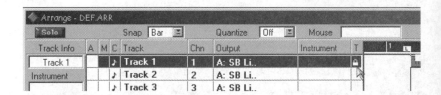

You can also use this procedure to create two pieces which run at different tempos. Why? Well, again, this may be required in film where one scene with music at one tempo fades into another scene with music at another tempo. The procedure is the same – record the first piece and Timelock the Tracks. Then insert a tempo change where the new piece begins – maybe a few bars before the first piece ends – and record the second piece.

Transferring tempo details between arrangements
There are two ways to transfer tempo events from one arrangement to another. As you probably know, several arrangements can be open at the same time. The Mastertrack editor works like the other editors and you can copy and paste tempo events, time signatures and hitpoints between arrangements.

You simply select the tempo events you want to copy, select another arrangement, set the Song Position to the point where you want to insert the events, and paste. Note that if any tempo data exists at the paste point, the new data will replace it.

This process enables you to transfer selected sections of a Mastertrack between arrangements.

To transfer an entire Mastertrack, use Export and Import in the Graphical Mastertrack editor. Export opens a standard file dialog box allowing you to save the Mastertrack. Import loads the Mastertrack into the current arrangement.

The Inspector

The Inspector is used to set playback parameter settings which affect Parts and Tracks during playback but which do not alter the data itself. It's great for making quick adjustments as the music is playing and many people use the Inspector as their main arranger and mixer.

With VST v4, Steinberg introduced additional Inspector parameters which give you even more control over playback, again without changing any of the data in the Tracks.

Writing Inspector parameters to the Tracks
The Inspector settings are saved with the song and as long as you load and play songs from within VST there's no need to physically insert the data into the Tracks.

However, if you want to edit the data in its playback format, say to edit a Part which has been transposed or whose velocity values have been changed, you need to apply the Inspector settings to the data. This is done simply by selecting Freeze Play Parameters from the Functions menu. The function is applied to all selected Parts or, if no individual Parts are selected, to all the Parts on the active Track.

Freezing parameters to create a MIDI file
When you export a MIDI file, you will usually want it to use the playback parameters you have set. It's not necessary to Freeze the parameters to do this. Instead, open the Preferences>MIDI>MIDI Files dialog and switch on the 'Include Part Parameters in Exported Files' option, Figure 7.1.

Item	State/Value
Explode Type 0 Files	On
Optimize Arrangement (only Type 1)	Off
Import Patches to Inspector	Off
Explode Files Dropped in Arrangement	On
Merge Mastertrack Events	On
Include Part Parameters in Exported Files	On
Don't import unknown Events	On

Figure 7.1 You can apply Inspector Parameters to MIDI files without freezing them first

INFO

See Chapter 17 for more about creating MIDI files.

A cautionary tale of freezing

The Freeze Play Parameters function inserts Bank Select, Program Change, Volume and Pan settings at the start of the Part or Parts. However, it inserts them all at the first event position. When the file plays back it will attempt to execute all the events at the same time which, of course, it can't do because MIDI is a serial protocol and the events are transmitted one after the other, even if they all have the same time position. However, it does transmit the data as fast as it possibly can.

In some situations and with some equipment, this can cause problems. Some gear takes a short while to react to Bank Select and Program Change messages for example, and data sent immediately after may be lost.

If you know that your gear works okay, that's fine, but if you are creating MIDI files for playing on a range of equipment, a safer option is to separate each item of data by a few ticks – 4 seems to be a fairly safe number.

Making all the Track parameters the same

When you're adjusting parameters in the Tracklist, you might want to make the same change to all the Tracks, say to set an initial volume or a MIDI output. You can do this with one stroke by holding down the Option key on the Mac or the Ctrl key on the PC while you make the change. (In versions of VST earlier than 4, this can be used to make all the MIDI Outputs the same.)

Easy General MIDI

If you're working with General MIDI files it's usually easier to select GM sounds by name rather than by Program Change number. VST has a ticky box to do just this. It's 'Use Inspector GM Names' and it's in the

Figure 7.2 Select GM sounds by name by checking this box

Figure 7.3 Click here to open the Inspector's extended parameters

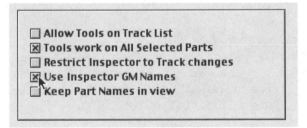

Preferences>General>Arrangement dialog, Figure 7.2. When this is checked a GM Name box appears in the Inspector allowing you to select sounds by name.

Big sounds with Multi Out

One of the Inspector's extended parameters is Multi Out. It works a little like Ghost Parts but with complete Tracks. It essentially lets you route a Track through a different set of Inspector settings. In fact, you can create as many Multi Outs as you wish, each with their own settings. (To open the extended Inspector area, click on the right arrow at the top of the Inspector window, Figure 7.3).

To create a Multi Out, click on the down arrow next to it, Figure 7.4. If this is the first Multi Out you've created, there will only be one option – Add Out, Figure 7.5. Select this and the Track name to the left will be preceded by the '&' symbol, Figure 7.6. The Multi Out menu now has options to delete the current Multi Out and to Mute it.

Figure 7.4 Select Multi Out from the drop-down menu

Figure 7.5 If this is the first Multi Out you've created there will only be one option

Figure 7.6 Default Multi Out Tracks have a '&' in front of them

You create other Multi Outs in the same way but they all appear with the '&' sign attached so it's a good idea to rename each one as you create them which you can do by double-clicking on the name.

When a Multi Out is selected, you can then change any of the Inspector parameters. Note, however, that if a Multi Out is on the same MIDI channel as the original (which it will be initially) there are certain parameters which cannot be changed, such as the main volume or the program number.

At its simplest, Multi Out lets you create a massive instrument stack simply by assigning several Multi Outs to different MIDI channels, each with a different sound. You could transpose a Multi Out to play an octave up or down from the original or to create any other harmony.

Quick staccato/legato

When you record a music part your performance usually takes into account the sound you are playing. If it sustains – vibes, for example – you are more likely to play in a slightly detached fashion because you don't have to hold the keys down so long as they continue to sound after releasing the key. When playing sounds with no sustain such as organ or trumpet, you probably hold down the keys to make sure the notes sound for their full duration.

That's fine and dandy but what happens if you decide that the brilliant flute line you've just recorded would sound better on piano or guitar? You don't have to re-record the part just to get the note lengths right, use the Length parameter in the Inspector. The range runs from 25 to 200%. At 25% the notes play for a quarter of their length, at 200% they play double their length. Adjust it to create a more legato or staccato playback.

Quick humanisation

Although there's no substitute for a part recorded live with bags of 'feel', if you have a pretty static part, perhaps recorded in step-time, you can humanise it a bit by varying the velocity and timing values. This is easily done in the Inspector's extended parameters section using the Randomise function.

There are two Random generators whose settings are applied to the selected Track or Part. Click the Off label and a small drop-down menu, Figure 7.7, shows the four parameters you can randomise – Position, Pitch, Velocity and Length. For the purposes of humanisation, the main ones of interest are Velocity coupled either with Position or Length. If you want to simulate the vagaries of inaccurate playing, too, by all means throw in Pitch.

Figure 7.7 You can randomise four parameters

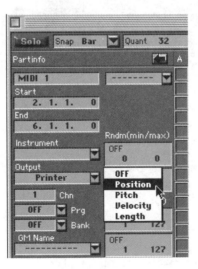

Depending on the part being humanised and how close its velocity values are, experiment with Velocity ranges of 10 to 20 or 30. If the range is too large the result will sound disjointed rather than human.

If the overall velocity seems to be too quiet or too loud, you can set most of the range in the minimum or maximum parameter – say from 10 to 20 to make the overall increase louder and from –20 to –10 to make it quieter.

Messing with Position is slightly more dodgy as this affects the timing of the notes. Try small adjustments and increase gradually. To create a 'push' or hurried effect, leave the minimum value at 0 and only raise the maximum value. For a lazy, held-back, behind the beat effect do it the other way around.

8

Editor tips

Moving around
In the major editors – Key, List, Score, Drum and Controller – you can move from event to event with the left and right cursor keys. In the Arrange page, too, you can move from Part to Part with the cursor keys. It's easier and faster than using the mouse.

QUICK TIP

You can open two or more editors simultaneously by holding down Shift as you open a new editor.

Opening editors
You can open any of the editors more quickly using hot keys than clicking on the menu option with the mouse.

Opening editors

PC	Mac	Opens
Ctrl E	Command E	Key (Audio editor if Audio Part selected)
Ctrl G	Command G	List
Ctrl D	Command D	Drum
Ctrl R	Command R	Score
Ctrl Y	N/A	GM/GS/XG editor
Ctrl B	Command B	Notepad
Ctrl L	Command L	Logical
Ctrl M	Command M	Graphical Mastertrack
Shift Ctrl M	Shift Command M	List Mastertrack

INFO

Remember - if you want to leave an editor without saving any of the changes you have made, press the Escape key.

Colour of music
If you're building up a complex arrangement, it can help to distinguish between Parts if you colour them. You can colour them by MIDI channel, by instrument name, by section (verse, chorus and so on) or by any other method you wish.

To colour a Part or Parts, simply select them by clicking on them while holding down Shift, then select a colour from the Part Color drop down menu at the top of the Arrange page, Figure 8.1. The menu already con-

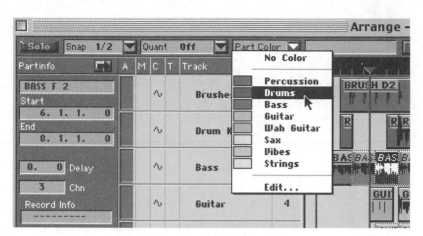

Figure 8.1 Select a colour from the drop-down menu

tains suggestions about what the colours could represent but you can change the names and add more if they don't suit your requirements.

Colour by Part

Apart from making it easier to see what the Parts are, colour can be used to differentiate between events in different Parts during editing.

Let's say you've coloured a number of Parts and you want to edit them. Select them and open the Key editor. Now select Colour by Parts from the Colour palette at the top right of the window, Figure 8.2. The events will now be coloured according to the colour of their parent Parts in the Arrange window, making them easier to identify.

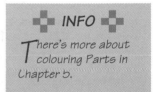

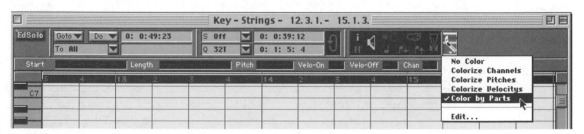

INFO

There's more about colouring Parts in Chapter 5.

Figure 8.2 Colour by Parts makes it easy to identify different Parts in the same editor

9

List editor tips

Filter tips

If a Part contains lots of different types of data such as Pitch Bend, Modulation, Controller data and Aftertouch as well as note data, it can sometimes be difficult to see the events you want to edit.

The Filter in the List editor lets you hide certain types of data. Click on the F in the function bar and a line of six data type will appear just above the event list, Figure 9.1. Clicking inside a box hides those events from the display making it easier to see and edit the other types of event.

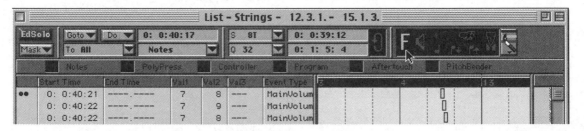

Figure 9.1 There are six Filter boxes just above the event list

Masking it

The Mask menu in List edit houses another filter option although its name can initially be confusing. It has two options - Mask It and Mask Event Type. If you highlight an event and select Mask It, the function hides all events which are not of the same type. So, if you highlight a note, Mask It would hide every other type of event from the list.

Mask Event Type goes a step further and shows not only events which are the same type but which also have the same Val 1 as the selected event. For notes, Val 1 is the pitch, for Controller events it is the type of Controller (the Controller number).

Mask or Filter?

The main difference between Mask and Filter is that Filtered events are still subject to editing. They may be hidden from view but they are not immune from processing.

If events are hidden using Mask, they are completely shielded both from view and from processing.

If you want to home in on a certain type of event to edit manually, then both systems can be very useful depending on what events you want to see. But use Mask to protect events when processing a Part, say with Logical edit.

Changing all events simultaneously

A common requirement in the List editor is to change selected events to the same value, say to set note velocities or Controller data to the same value. This is easily done by holding down Alt on the PC or Option on the Mac while changing the value with the mouse.

Note positions by time or length

In the List editor, note information is usually shown as a Start Position and a Length, Figure 9.2. However, by clicking on the box which shows the mouse position, this changes to Start Time and End Time, Figure 9.3. This is an extremely useful display if events have to occur at a specific time as is common in film work.

This also works with audio events, making it extremely easy to move an audio event to a specific time, again useful in film work.

Start-Pos.	Length	Val.1	Val.2	Val.3	Status
0001.01.096	576	C3	127	64	Note
0001.03.192	672	D3	127	64	Note
0002.01.192	768	E3	127	64	Note
0002.03.192	768	F#3	127	64	Note
0003.01.192	864	A3	127	64	Note
0003.04.000	672	G3	127	64	Note
0004.01.192	768	E3	127	64	Note

Figure 9.2 Notes are usually shown as a Start Position and Length ...

Start-Time	End-Time	Val.1	Val.2	Val.3
00:00:00:03	00:00:00:21	C3	127	64
00:00:01:06	00:00:02:03	D3	127	64
00:00:02:06	00:00:03:06	E3	127	64
00:00:03:06	00:00:04:06	F#3	127	64
00:00:04:06	00:00:05:09	A3	127	64
00:00:05:12	00:00:06:09	G3	127	64
00:00:06:06	00:00:07:06	E3	127	64

Figure 9.3 ... but can be shown as Start Time and End Time

10
Drum programming tips

Recording drums

The Drum editor makes it very easy to create, edit and generally mess around with drum patterns. However, it is the equivalent of a step-time editor and the notes all sit nicely on the beat and have fixed velocity values (although you can change and edit these, of course).

For a more natural feel, try recording the drums from a keyboard in real-time. Record it in sections, say the intro, verse and chorus, rather than simply recording one bar and then copying and pasting it. You'll get a better feel this way.

Also, rather than laying down one drum at a time, record two or more drums at once. In fact, it's usually easier to do this than to record one drum at a time! Bass and snare lines, for example, generally go together very well – unless you're writing complex Trip Hop stuff! – as the two drums create their own rhythm. This actually makes it easier to 'get in the groove' than playing one drum at a time which is like trying to play half a rhythm.

Just as bass and snare often go together, so do open and closed hi hats, toms, congas and bongos, and several other topping-type drums.

How to create a drum map

In order to use the Drum editor to its full, you need to configure it to your drum set. This means making a drum map. It is easy to do but many people are put off because of the time it can take. However, once you have created it, you'll find it much easier to work with drum patterns in the future.

Before you embark on the process of creating your own drum map, see if there is already a drum map for your instrument in the Drum Maps folder. This should have been copied to your hard disk when you installed VST but you may want to check the original CD to make sure all the files have been copied across.

If a drum map you want is not there, it's worth checking to see if there's one on the Web. Check the Cubase and Steinberg sites and the site of your instrument's manufacturer (see Appendix 3, page 152) for useful Web sites).

The Autoload song loads with a GM drum map and is automatically installed in the Library Files folder, Figure 10.1, so if you use only GM

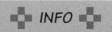

INFO

To make a Track a Drum class Track, click on its C column and select Drum Track from the pop-up menu.

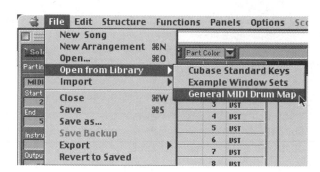

Figure 10.1 You can quickly load the GM drum map using the Library option

you may think you don't need to mess with the map but take a look at 'Optimising drum map layouts' which comes up in the section after next.

The Drum editor is designed to be used with Drum class Tracks. You can open a normal MIDI Track in the Drum editor but it won't have all the Drum Track parameters.

So, to create a new drum map you can start with a map which is similar to the one you want and edit it or you can start with a blank slate.

Drum column parameters

M	Mutes the drum.
Drum Name	The name of the drum which you enter when creating the drum map.
Q	Quantize value, where the note is placed when you enter it on the grid. It's the equivalent of the Snap value in other editors but you can have different Q settings for each drum. The Q setting is only used when you create notes. When you apply regular quantization, the setting on the Status bar is used and when you move a note the Snap value is used.
I-Note	The Input note. When VST receives this note – if you play it on a keyboard, for example – the sound is triggered.
Len	The length of the note when you enter it on the grid. Most drum sounds are 'one shot' sounds and only need a 'trigger' note which can be very short indeed. Once triggered the drum sound will usually play in its entirety. The length, then, is usually irrelevant although some drum units, particularly older ones, may need a note of a certain length in order to recognise it. Try a value of 8 or 16 and increase it if the drum unit does not respond.
O-Note	The Output note. When the sound is triggered, this is the note the program transmits. In other words this is the actual note number of the drum sound.
Instrument	An additional naming option should you wish to use it.
Chn	The MIDI channel the sound is transmitted on.
Output	The MIDI output the sound is transmitted to. One drum map can output through several MIDI Outs.
Diamonds	There are four diamonds which represent different velocity values used when entering notes. The default values are 70, 90, 110 and 120.
Delay	This shifts the timing of the note backwards or forwards. It can be useful to compensate for timing variations if you are using sounds from different instruments in the same drum map although this shouldn't be necessary with modern instruments. It can also be used for special rhythmic effects, say to push or pull a snare line to give the pattern more drive or more of a laid-back feel.

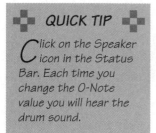

✦ QUICK TIP ✦

*Click on the Speaker
icon in the Status
Bar. Each time you
change the O-Note
value you will hear the
drum sound.*

To create a drum map, for each drum you must enter the O-Note and then the I-Note note names. In most cases these will be the same. In a GM kit, for example, C1 triggers the bass drum and D1 triggers the snare. Where things can get more complex is if the I-Note and O-Note settings are not the same.

What's the benefit of this? Sticking with the GM drum set, let's say you want to record a Latin American pattern with bass, snare, congas and bongos. If, like many musicians, you record drum parts by playing them on a keyboard, you'll find that the congas and bongos are in the third octave of the keyboard, well away from the bass and snare.

What you can do is change the conga and bongo I-Notes so that they are triggered by keys closer to the bass and snare. An example – the hi bongo is normally C3, but if its I-Note was changed to E1, for example, than E1 would trigger the note, Figure 10.2. In other words, E1 is 'mapped' to C3, which is where the 'map' in 'drum map' comes from.

Figure 10.2 You can change the note that triggers a drum sound by remapping it

Each sound must have its own I-Note and if you try to select an I-Note which is already in use, the program will pop-up a warning message.

Instead of physically typing in the O-Note, you can record it from a MIDI keyboard by switching on the MIDI icon in the Status bar. With the drum line highlighted, playing a note on the keyboard will enter the note name into the line.

Using non-drum sounds in a drum map

As hinted in the previous section, all the drums do not have to be on the same MIDI channel or even assigned to the same MIDI output. By changing the MIDI channel you could use sounds in the standard voice section of an instrument, and by using a different MIDI output you can play sounds on another instrument, perhaps a sampler.

There are percussion sounds in the normal GM voice set which could be added to a drum map. Also, try pressing other instruments into service as drums particularly at very low or high pitches.

When using non-drum sounds, the Len parameter will assume a greater importance.

Optimising drum map layouts

If you work with pre-programmed drum maps you may often find that the drums you use the most are spread throughout the list and you have to scroll through the display to find your favourite selection of bass, snare, toms and hi hats. But you don't have to.

If you click and hold on a drum name you can drag it up and down to a new position in the list. This lets you put the drums you use most frequently together for faster and easier access. You can even create different layouts to suit different types of music – one for rock, one for Latin, and so on.

Creating drum echoes

Spice up your drum parts by adding a little echo to some of the drums. This is most easily done by splitting a drum Track into its component drum notes, creating Ghost Parts of selected drum sounds and delaying them a little.

To split a drum Part into its components drums, highlight the Part or Track then select Explode by Channel or Remix (depending on which version of VST you have) from the Structure menu.

Drag the Ghost parts to the right, say by 1/16th note – this is easily done by selecting a 1/16 Snap value – and use the Velocity parameter in the Inspector to reduce the volume of the two Tracks, Figure 10.3.

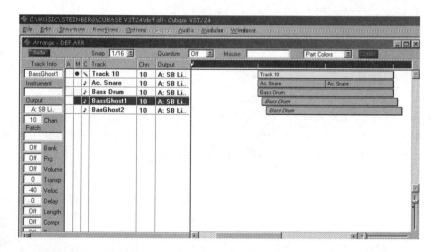

Figure 10.3 Create drum echoes by clicking and dragging

This can be very effective with all sorts of drums from bass and snare lines to ethnic percussion.

Echo round the bones

You can create even more interesting, complex and intricate patterns by running a drum line through the MIDI Processor. In some versions of VST this may be found in the Modules menu, in others it has its own MIDI Processor entry in the Options menu or MIDI Echo/Pitch Shift entry in the Panels menu. Whatever version you have, the basic operating principle is the same.

Figure 10.4 Route the drum
Track to the MIDI Echo
Processor

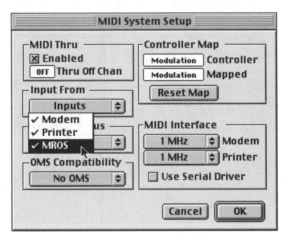

The first step is to route the drum Track to the processor. This may mean selecting MROS as the output for the Track or, if using the MIDI Echo/Pitch Shift processor, select the Echo output, Figure 10.4.

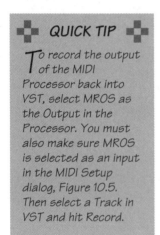

QUICK TIP

To record the output of the MIDI Processor back into VST, select MROS as the Output in the Processor. You must also make sure MROS is selected as an input in the MIDI Setup dialog, Figure 10.5. Then select a Track in VST and hit Record.

Figure 10.5 Route the Echo output back into VST

Make the processor active, set the output and MIDI channel and then play with the controls, Figure 10.6. A suggested starting point might be:

Repeat	3
Echo	24
Quantize	1
Vel Dec	−16
Echo Dec	0
Note Dec	0

Figure 10.6 Suggested
starting values for the MIDI
Echo Processor

There are a few interesting controls to dabble with. Vel Dec adds or sub-tracts a velocity from each echo. Using a short Echo value (24 sets 1/8th note delays, 12 sets 1/16th note delays) with a lot of repeats and decay-ing velocities you can create some super rolling snare patterns.

Even more interesting is Note Dec which adds or subtracts a value to or from the note number of the echoes. Using a single drum note as the core pattern, this will trigger additional drum sounds. It's not exactly ran-dom drum selection and it can produce some surprisingly interesting drum lines.

For a more subtle effect, use a very long Echo time to introduce more sparse hits to the pattern.

Score editor tips

Cubase VST has a Score editor which is quite adequate for editing notes on the stave. Many users who read the dots prefer working with notation rather than the Key editor display because it's easier to recognise the music from notation than it is from a piano roll display.

Cubase VST Score, however, has many additional features specifically designed for adjusting the layout and formatting the score for printing.

Edit mode vs. Page mode

Figure 11.1 Edit mode (left) and Figure 11.2 Page mode (right) give you two ways to look at and edit a score

The Score editor has two modes – Edit, Figure 11.1, and Page, Figure 11.2, selected from the Score menu. You can perform all edit functions in both modes so why use Edit mode at all?

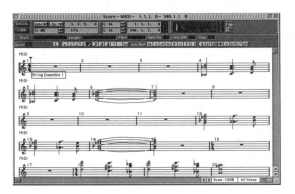

If you are simply using the dots to edit notes and not to prepare a score for printing, use Edit mode. It scrolls, like the other editors, from left to right (Page mode scrolls vertically) and it doesn't encumber you with unwanted layout Tools – which you won't want if you're not creating a layout!

If you are producing a score for printing then Page mode is the mode to use. You may well have to change some notes in order for the layout to look good and this could well spoil playback so when preparing a score for printing, always work with a copy.

Quick clicks

You can select notes by clicking, holding down Shift while clicking in order to select non-contiguous notes, and by dragging a selection box over them as you can in the other editors. Here are some other shortcuts:

- Holding down Ctrl on the PC or Command on the Mac and double-clicking on a note selects all notes of that pitch.
- Holding down Alt on the PC or Option on the Mac and double-clicking on a note selects all notes of the same name at all octaves.
- Double-clicking on a note head opens a Note Info box, Figure 11.3, which lets you change various attributes of the notes including making it a grace note.

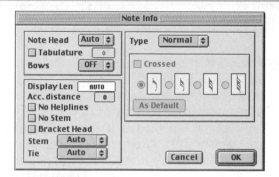

Figure 11.3 The Note Info box presents a range of attributes for editing

In fact, double-clicking on most symbols, clefs, bar lines, time signatures, text and so on, opens up an Info box where changes and selections can be made.

Preventing pitch and time slips

You can click and drag notes around the score to change their pitch and time position but it's very easy to change both of these when you only want to change one.

The solution is to hold down Shift before moving the note. If the first movement is vertical, you will not then be able to move the note horizontally and vice versa. After moving a note, release the mouse button before the Shift key. You can move several notes in this way by Shift-clicking to select them.

Display Quantize

When preparing a score for printing, in order to line up the notes on suitable divisions of the beat, one of the first stops should be the Display Quantize settings in the Staff Settings dialog, Figure 11.4, selected from the Score menu.

The most important thing to realise is that the Display Quantize settings only affect the way the score looks in the Score editor and when printed out. The actual timing of the note data is not changed.

If the music contains regular note lengths such as 1/4, 1/8 or 1/16 notes, you ought to be able to get pretty close to a final layout using just the Notes and Rests settings. These specify the smallest note and rest values that will be displayed. There are triplet settings here, too, Figure 11.5, which you use, obviously, if the score contains triplets.

The Auto Quant box should be checked only if the score contains a mix of 'straight' notes and triplets, otherwise leave it unchecked. The two boxes below this help find errant triplets. If the score contains perfect

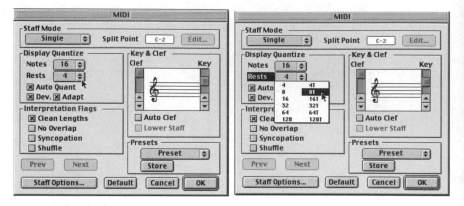

Figure 11.4 (left) and Figure 11.5 The Display Quantize dialog controls the way the score looks on the screen

Figure 11.6 Clean lengths can fix problems with short rests

triplets (if they have been entered in step-time or the Part quantized) then you should not need to use them.

When checked, the Dev (Deviation) box tries to detect triplets even if they deviate slightly from the beat they ought to be on. The Adapt box 'guesses' that where there's one triplet, others are lurking nearby. If the previous settings do not detect all the triplets in the score, turn this on.

The Interpretation Flags are used to tidy up other aspects of the score.

Clean Lengths adjusts the lengths of notes to remove small rests which can appear between notes which are just a wee bit shorter than they should be. Figure 11.6 shows before and after versions of a slightly-short 1/8th note.

No Overlap removes ties which can occur when notes which start at the same position have different lengths. This is illustrated in Figure 11.7 which shows the notes as recorded in the Key editor, how they appear in the Score editor and then how they appear after No Overlap has been switched on.

Syncopation is particularly useful with swing and jazz music. When it is off, the program usually adds ties to notes which cross beats. It's often easier to read, however, if the notes are simply given their correct durations, and this format is often preferred in modern arrangements. Figure 11.8 shows how Syncopation changes the display.

Finally, Shuffle is again useful with modern music, jazz in particular. It's quite common to score a swing or shuffle as straight notes and put a comment at the top of the score to the effect that they should be played

Figure 11.7 No overlap removes unwanted ties when notes which start at the same time have different lengths

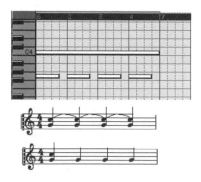

Figure 11.8 The Syncopation setting makes swing arrangements easier to read

in swing fashion. Straight notes are easier to read and it's a common shorthand which makes the music more legible. VST's Shuffle function looks for occurrences of a quarter-note triplet followed by an eighth-note triplet (or corresponding eighth and sixteenth notes) and displays them as regular straight notes, Figure 11.9.

Figure 11.9 The Shuffle function displays swing timings as straight notes

The Display Quantize Tool

It sometimes happens that one Display Quantize setting will not correctly display an entire score. Enter the Display Quantize Tool which can be used to enter new settings at any point in the score. Select the Tool from the Toolbox and click on the score where the new settings are required and an Insert Quantize dialog appears, Figure 11.10, where you can enter new settings.

Figure 11.10 The Display Quantize function can fix small groups of notes

If you only need to apply this quantization to a few bars you can enter the length in the Length box or use the Tool to click at the point where the settings are no longer required and click on the Restore To Staff button.

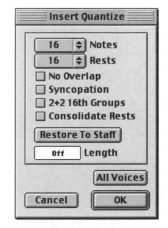

Manual adjustments

Occasionally you may come across or create a score which simply cannot be displayed satisfactorily using the Display Quantize function. In this case you may well have to resort to editing the notes themselves. Good job you made a backup isn't it?

What layout?

VST has a mass of options for creating score layouts. But before you start creating your own, check in the Library, Scores and Layouts folders to see what preset layouts have been supplied with the program.

How do you load them? It's a well-guarded secret. With the Score editor open, select Page mode from the Score menu, then select Score>Format>Page Mode Settings. Click on the Load button and navigate your way to the Layouts folder.

Logical editor tips

The Logical editor is one of VST's most powerful features. It can literally transform one type of MIDI data into another and perform a whole range of useful and powerful edit functions.

Some of the functions Logical edit was used for can be done in other ways in VST v4. For example, randomising note velocities and position to 'humanise' a line can be done with the Random functions in the Inspector's extended parameter area. However, Logical edit can do much more than that and this chapter contains some suggested applications.

The Logical editor is selected from the Functions menu.

Easy vs. Expert mode

The Expert mode adds two additional Filter and Processing columns and five more processing operators to the Value 1 and Value 2 columns. Expert mode doesn't make the layout look that much more complicated and the additional operators can suggest ways of processing data which you may not have considered. Be a power user and say no to Easy mode.

Saving and organising your Presets

In v4, VST stores Logical edit Presets as files on disk in the Logical Presets folder (although you can change the location from Functions> Logical>Show List if you wish). The program comes with a collection of Presets grouped into two folders called Standard Set 1 and Standard Set 2. You can add new folders here and copy Preset files into them. It is, therefore, very easy to create folders of specific functions, and even folders of functions for use with specific projects.

Dynamic panning

Logical edit is particularly good at manipulating Controller data so let's see what we can do with Pan.

Like many aspects of VST, there is often more than one way to achieve a result. For example, in the following example you could include the pan data in the same Part as the note data using Logical edit's Insert, but there are advantages to keeping them separate – for one, it's easier and faster to delete the Controller Part if you make a pig's ear of it and start again than it is to remove selected data from it.

The following dynamic pan procedure was developed to add more interest to piano parts. Although the piano is a stereo instrument, the

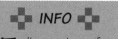

QUICK TIP

The Menu References document contains details of all the preset, er, Presets supplied with VST.

INFO

Earlier versions of VST saved the Logical edit Presets with the Song, so if you have an earlier version, after creating new Presets, save the Song.

stereo spread is not usually very great and most piano parts in MIDI recordings are in mono. What we do here is assign a pan position to every note so the lower the note, the further left it is panned and the higher the note, the further right it is panned.

Take a piano Part, copy it and place it below the original on another Track set to the same MIDI channel. Select the copy and open the Logical editor. We now convert the note data to pan data.

In the Filter section, set the Event Type to Note. Ignore the other columns. In the Processing section Fix the Event Type to Control Change. This converts the notes to Controller data. Select Fix in the Value 1 column and set this to 10 which is Pan's Controller number. Now we want to use the note's MIDI number (Value 1) for the Pan position so in the Value 2 column select Value 1 from the pop-up menu.

Finally, we'll move the Pan events back a little to give them time to kick in before the note sounds so set Minus 4 in the Position column. Make sure Quantize is Off, set the Function to Transform then click on Do It. You can see the setup in Figure 12.1.

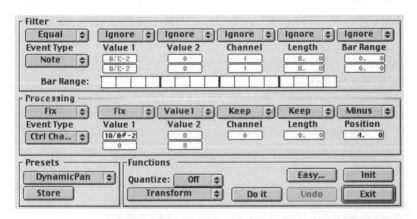

Figure 12.1 The dynamic pan set-up

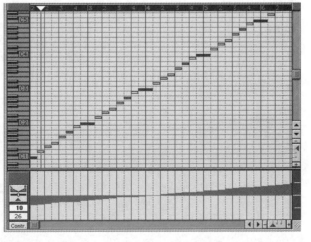

Figure 12.2 Each note has a corresponding pan event

You will end up with a set of Pan data which corresponds to the note pitches as in Figure 12.2. You can keep the Parts separate or merge them. Remember to store the Preset 'cause you'll need it for the Big Pan...

Big Pan

You'll notice than in the previous example in Figure 12.2 that the notes only cover a five-octave pitch range and the Pan events, therefore, do not pan any of the notes very far either way. The fact is, most instruments do not have a great pitch range – the piano has one of the largest although few piano pieces make use of the full range.

So, if you want to make a meal out of it, you can create an even broader pan range, stretching from 0 right through to 127. The first step is to find the lowest and highest notes. Let's say these are note numbers 36 (C1) and 95 (B5). In Logic edit, subtract the lowest note number from all the notes, Figure 12.3.

Figure 12.3 The first step in creating a really Big Pan

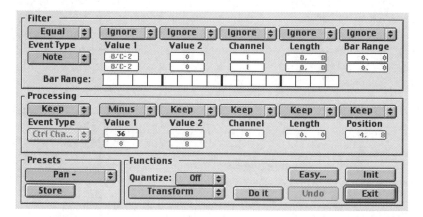

Calculate the resulting highest value (in this case it will be 95 – 36 = 59). Now divide 127 by this figure (127/59 = 2.15) and multiply Value 1 by this, Figure 12.4. Then use the Dynamic Pan Preset you created in the previous example. The result will be a set of Pan data which covers most of the range from 0 to 127, Figure 12.5.

Figure 12.4 The second step in creating a Big Pan

You can do with this any piece of music, of course, not just piano parts. One interesting experiment is to Big Pan every instrument in an

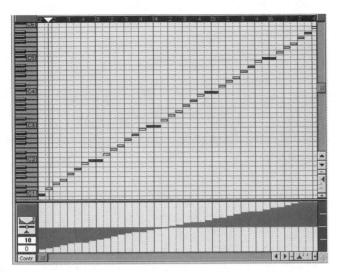

arrangement which can result in the individual sounds panning wildly around the stereo image. Try it with *Flight of the Bumble Bee...*

Autopan

In the previous examples, each music line must be processed individually. You can also create generic functions which can be applied to any piece of music. Here we'll create an Autopan.

The first step is to create some Pan data. In the Arrange page create a Part one bar long. Open the List editor, set the Event Type to Controller, the Snap value to 16 and select Fill from the Do menu. The Part will now contain 16 Bank Select messages. Change the Val1 column to 10 to turn them into Pan data, Figure 12.6. You can change all the columns simultaneously by holding down Option on the Mac or Alt on the PC while changing the value with the mouse. We use this as a core Part for creating the effects so copy it because we'll be using it more than once.

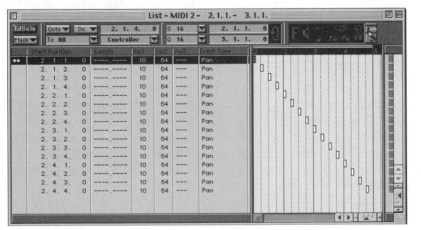

Figure 12.6 Filling a Part with pan data

First we'll create a left/right pan. In the Logical editor set the Filter to Equal Control Change and Value 1 to 10. In the Processing section set all the columns to Keep except Value 2 and set that to Dyn. Set the range from 0 to 127, Figure 12.7.

Figure 12.7 Creating a left/right pan

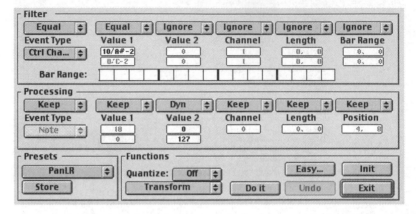

Now use another core Part. The settings are exactly the same except the Dyn range is reversed, Figure 12.8. This produces a pan from right to left.

Figure 12.8 Creating a right/left pan

You can then copy and position the two pan Parts one after the other to create left/right pan sweeps, Figure 12.9.

As it stands it takes a bar to sweep from left to right and another bar to sweep back gain. You can create faster and slower sweeps very easily using Presets which come with VST. Merge four of the Parts to create a pan Part as in Figure 12.9. Now in Logical edit, select the Double Speed, Figure 12.10, and/or the Half Speed, Figure 12.11, Presets and apply them to the Autopan Part. The Double Speed Preset will make a complete left/right sweep occur in one bar instead of two, Figure 12.12. You can apply the Presets more than once for even faster – or slower – pans.

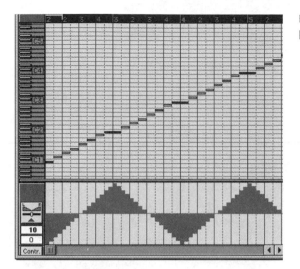

Figure 12.9 Using four pan parts to create pan sweeps

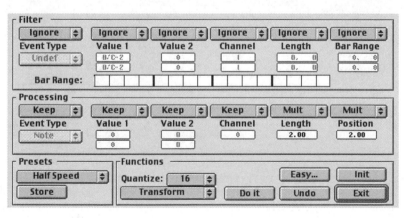

Figure 12.10 The Double Speed preset

Figure 12.11 The Half Speed Preset

Figure 12.12 Applying the
Double Speed preset to the
Autopan Part doubles the
speed of the pan

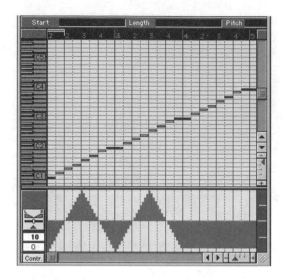

AutoTremolo

Now that we have an Autopan Part, it's easy to convert the Pan data into another type of data. If it's converted to Volume data the result will be AutoTremolo instead of Autopan. To be most effective the tremolo should be faster than the pan, say four or more cycles per bar.

Only one setting needs to be made in Logical edit and that's in the Processing section. Set Value 1 to Fix with a value of 7 which is Volume's Controller number, Figure 12.13. The Pan events will change to Volume.

Figure 12.13 Creating an Auto
Tremolo effect

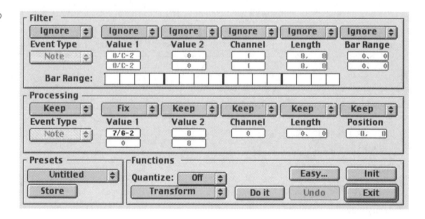

This setting runs the full volume range from 0 to 127 and with a slow tremolo the sound may fade completely for too long. You can change this by increasing the Volume values by, say, 30 or 40 – set Value 2 to Plus 40.

Other sweeping applications

Hopefully, you will now be thinking of other applications and processes. You can program pitch bend and modulation sweeps and ramps and if you have an instrument which responds to real-time Controller changes you could create a sweep which would change the filter in real-time. We'll leave that to the more adventurous...

Gate effects

Using the principles described above, you can use the Logical editor to create gate effects by converting notes into Volume data and setting their values to create rhythmic effects. You could even set the values to random and see what emerges. There's a little more about creating gate effects in Chapter 14.

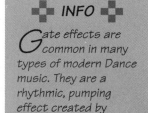

INFO

Gate effects are common in many types of modern Dance music. They are a rhythmic, pumping effect created by rapidly turning the volume of a sound up and down or on and off.

13

Audio tips

Quick audio import

You don't have to load audio files via the Audio Pool. You can import audio directly into the Arrange page on the current Track at the Left Locator position. The Import Audio function is in the File menu.

You can also open an audio file directly into the Audio editor by clicking in it with the Pencil Tool.

Dynamic events for Volume

Although there's a certain *je ne sais quois* about doing a real-time mix with the faders, you can achieve more accurate and precise control over volume by using dynamic events.

Double-click on an audio Part to open the Audio editor. In the View menu, enable Dynamic Events and the waveform display will lift leaving a blank area beneath it, Figure 13.1. If you can't see a waveform, make sure the Waveforms entry in the View menu is also enabled.

Figure 13.1 If you want to see Dynamic Events you must enable the option first

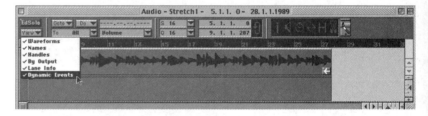

Click on the pop-up menu to the right of the 'To' menu (it's not clearly named in the manual), Figure 13.2, and select Volume. A line will appear near the top of the lower part of the event which indicates the volume level. If it doesn't look like that there must already be some Volume events on the Track.

Figure 13.2 Select Volume as a dynamic event

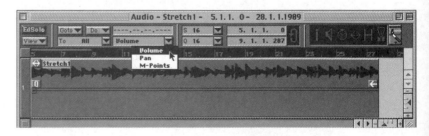

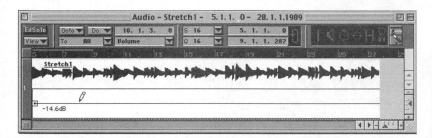

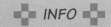

Figure 13.3 Dragging the volume line shows the level in dB

Select the Pencil Tool, click on the line and drag it up and down to change the volume. The level in dB appears next to the node as you move it, Figure 13.3.

Hold Down Alt on the PC or Option on the Mac and click with the Pencil on the line. Another node appears and you can continue clicking to create as many nodes as you wish, Figure 13.4. If you get carried away, you can delete nodes with the Eraser.

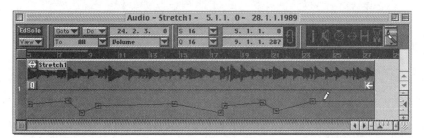

Figure 13.4 Click with the Pencil to create nodes for dragging

You can now drag the nodes around the editor to create a volume envelope which can be as complex as you wish. This is far more precise than using the mixer. You can drawn in long fades, create sharp volume changes and even draw in tremolo curves, Figure 13.5, although you will need to zoom in on the audio file to do this.

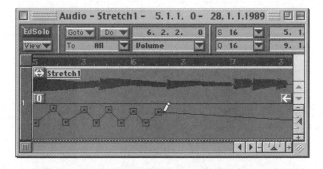

Figure 13.5 You can create tremolo curves by dragging the nodes

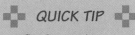
Dynamic events for Pan

Dynamic Pan events can be created and edited in exactly the same way. Select Pan from the same drop-down menu that Volume is on and create and edit nodes with the Pencil Tool.

You can position specific sections of audio at different parts of the stereo image and draw in envelopes to create autopan effects.

Use zero crossing points

As most readers will be aware, when you cut a couple of sections of audio and try to splice them together there's a good chance the join may click during playback. This happens if the two signals have different volume levels at the join which creates a sharp change in the signal level know as a transient. If the waveform in Figure 13.6 was cut and spliced at the points shown, a click would inevitably result.

Figure 13.6 Cutting and splicing at these points would create a click at the join

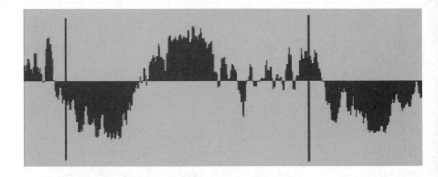

Figure 13.7 Cutting audio at these points is less likely to produce a click

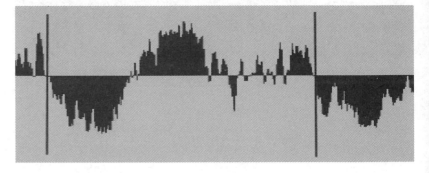

The way to avoid this is to cut the waveform at zero crossing points where the waveform crosses the central axis at which point they are at 'zero' voltage, Figure 13.7. You can get VST to do this for you by switching on Options>Audio Setup>Snap To Zero, Figure 13.8. When this is on, the following operations will occur at the nearest zero crossing points to the positions selected:

Splitting events in the Audio editor
Using Snip Loop in the Audio editor
Changing Start and End Insets
Using Banish Silence in the Audio editor and the Pool
Splitting Parts in the Arrange window

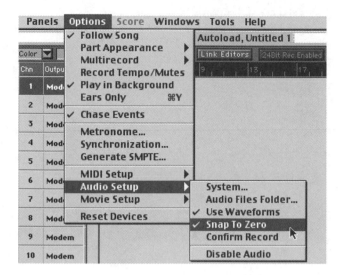

Figure 13.8 Select this to make VST use zero crossing points

Removing clicks

It's not an uncommon experience to discover that a carefully made recording has a click in it. Clicks often occur in material which has been copied to hard disk from other media, particularly vinyl. If you work a lot with material containing clicks and other unwanted noise, your best bet is to invest in an audio restoration program or a declicking plug-in (see next section). However, if you only need to remove the odd click or two, here's a way to do it in VST.

Figure 13.9 shows a recording in the Audio editor with a couple of spikes in the middle. Open the Wave editor by double-clicking in the Audio editor. You can also open it by selecting the audio in the Audio editor and then selecting Edit from the Edit menu (in some versions of VST you may need to access Edit Audio from the Audio menu).

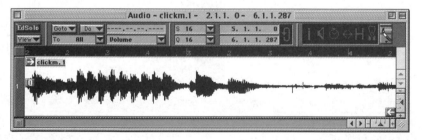

Figure 13.9 A recording containing clicks

PC users can use an external editor such as WaveLab by setting it up in the Audio Preferences dialog, Figure 13.10. The example here assumes you are using the internal editor.

Highlight the offending spike and zoom in on it, Figure 13.11. You may have to keep reselecting the area and zooming in on it to get up close and personal. When you're fully zoomed in, highlight just the offending click, Figure 13.12.

Figure 13.10 PC users can
select an external audio
editor of their choice

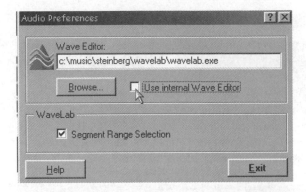

Figure 13.11 The first step to
removing a spike is to zoom
in on it

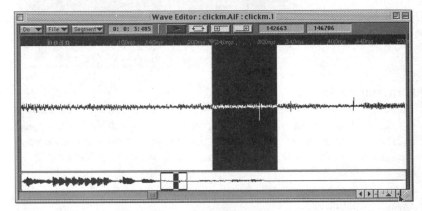

Figure 13.12 Highlight the
offending material

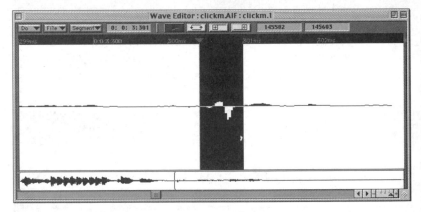

You now have three options. You can simply delete the section using Cut from the Edit menu. If you have enabled Snap To Zero (see previous section) this ought to produce a good result but this does reduce the size of the recording and even a few samples may have a detrimental effect on the timing.

The second option is to use Quieten from the Do menu. Run it a few times until the spike shrinks and see if that fixes it.

The third option is to replace the section containing the spike with another section. Select the Hand Tool and move the selected area across the waveform, left or right, to a section which is click-free. Copy it, then paste it over the click.

Declickers and denoisers

If you regularly work with noisy material or if you transfer vinyl – or older! – recordings to CD, you may need some extra help. Fortunately, there are several plug-ins which de-noise, de-click, de-crackle and de-hum recordings.

Steinberg has two useful plug-ins. DeNoiser, Figure 13.13, removes broadband noise such as that caused by equipment hum and noisy fans. It uses an adaptive process which automatically detects changes in noise levels and makes changes to the audio accordingly. The DeClicker detects clicks and 'redraws' the audio material beneath them.

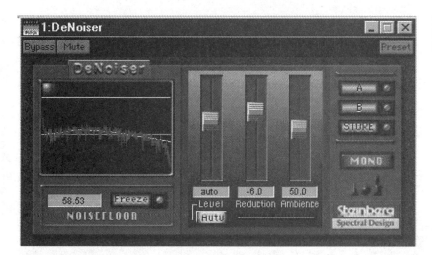

Figure 13.13 Steinberg's DeNoiser Plug-in removes broadband noise

Sonic Foundry's Noise Reduction plug-in, Figure 13.14, (currently only available for the PC) tackles both noise reduction and click removal. It adopts a different approach to the DeNoiser and takes a spectral fingerprint – or noiseprint – of the background noise (you need a music-free section containing just the noise to do this) which it removes from the rest of the recording.

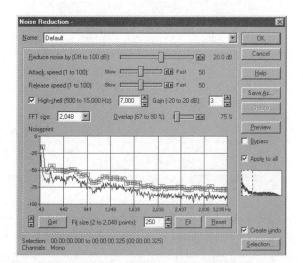

Figure 13.14 Sonic Foundry's Noise Reduction Plug-in uses a spectral fingerprint to remove noise

Then there's Arboretum's Ray Gun which is easy to use with sliders to control noise reduction, pops, crackles and hum.

You will find utilities such as these indispensable in your war against noise. They can remove unwanted sound material far better and easier than is possible by manual editing or EQ techniques.

Fitting tempo to a sample loop

A popular method of song construction is to use sample loops for the backing and add additional parts – MIDI and audio – over the top. There are hundreds of commercial sample loop CDs catering for virtually every type of music.

The basic process in VST is to import a few sample loops and arrange them on Tracks in the Arrange page. However, not all sample CDs include the tempo the loops were recorded at, and one or two which do have been known to be a little less than exact. This tip explains how to set the tempo to match that of a loop.

First import the loop. You can load it into the Audio Pool and drag it to a Track or you can import it directly onto an audio Track using the File>Import>Audio File option. Drag it to a suitable music position. If it starts on a downbeat, that would be the beginning of a bar. Figure 13.15 shows an eight-bar drum loop which doesn't quite fit the eight bars at the default tempo of 120bpm.

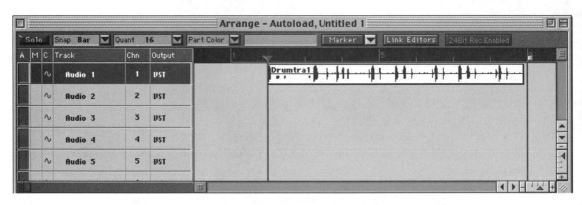

Figure 13.15 This eight-bar drum loop doesn't quite fit the eight bars

Double-click on it to open the Audio editor. Drag across the timeline at the top of the editor to set the length of time that you want the loop to occupy. This will be a little longer or shorter than the sample. In this case it's from bars 2 to 9, Figure 13.16. Set the Snap value to make sure you get the length exact.

Figure 13.16 Drag across the timeline for the full eight bars

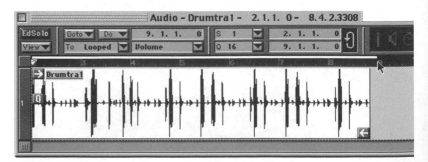

Select the loop by clicking on it then select Fit Event to Loop Range from the Do menu. A dialog box pops up asking if you want to fit the audio to the loop by adjusting the tempo or the audio. Click on the Tempo button and the tempo will change as you'll see in the Transport Bar, Figure 13.17.

Figure 13.17 The tempo has changed to make the audio fit its allotted eight bars

When creating a song with both sample loops and MIDI recordings, start the song with the sample loops and use a tempo which fits them. It's easier than starting with MIDI backing tracks and then trying to make the audio fit the tempo. Although you can do that as we see next...

Making sample loops fit a tempo

Sometimes you may want to add a sample loop to an existing recording but the loop has been recorded at a different tempo. This calls for a spot of timestretching.

Proceed as in the previous example but when the dialog box asks if you want to Fit by Tempo or Audio, click on the Audio button. This will timestretch the audio to fit the loop made in the Audio editor's timeline rather than change the tempo to fit the audio.

You can use this process in order to incorporate several sample loops which have been recorded at different tempos in the same song.

The reason why it is usually recommended that samples are imported first rather than being timestretched later is because timestretch does invariably alter the quality of the recording, and also, it is far easier to change the tempo of a MIDI recording.

Re-Grooving an audio recording

If you like messing around with sample loops then Steinberg's ReCycle, Figure 13.18, is the program for you. With it you can chop an audio file into its component parts and play them in a different order or at a different tempo. You can do a similar thing in VST albeit in a much more limited way.

The process works best on drum loops or at least with files which have well-defined 'hits'. Load the loop and open it in the Audio editor. Highlight it, make sure Dynamic Events are selected in the View menu, and select Get M-Points from the Do menu.

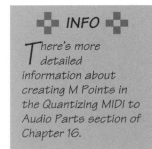

INFO

There's more detailed information about creating M Points in the Quantizing MIDI to Audio Parts section of Chapter 16.

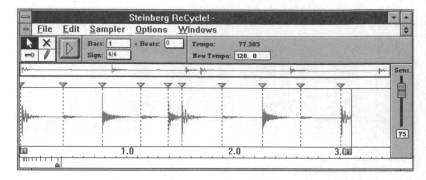

Figure 13.18 Steinberg's
ReCycle lets you play fast
and loose with sample loops

You may want to add or remove M Points which you can do manually
or by running the Get M-Point process again and adjusting the parameters. The object is to divide the loop into its component parts or hits. In
Figure 13.19, for example, there are two M Points close together in the
middle of the loop and you may want to remove the second one.

Figure 13.19 M-Points pick up
on volume highs in the audio

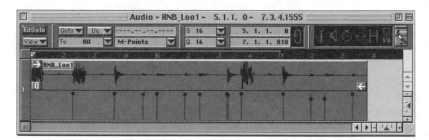

Next, with the audio still highlighted, select Snip at M-Points from the
Do menu, Figure 13.20. You'll now find you can increase and decrease
the tempo and the loop will play faster or slower. Neat uh?

Figure 13.20 Snip at
M-Points cuts the audio into
sections

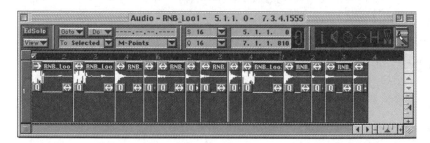

However, this does have its limitations. If you slow down the tempo
too much the segments will space out and the groove will sound as if it's
stuttering, Figure 13.21. Likewise, if you speed it up too much, the segments will overlap each other and will probably not play properly, either.
But as a quick fix it's useful if you don't have ReCycle.

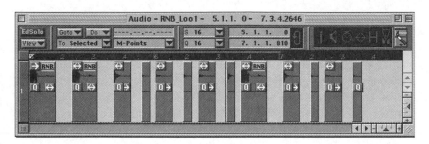

Figure 13.21 If you slow down the tempo too much there will be gaps between the audio sections

Quantizing audio Parts

Once you've snipped an audio Part into segments with Snip at M-Points (see previous section), you can quantize it. Again, if this puts too much space between events, the results may not be very good.

You can also quantize a Part by timestretching it. This processes the audio file itself so you may want to make a copy of it before you start. You can easily and quickly duplicate an audio file in the Audio Pool using the Duplicate File option in its File menu.

Mac users have the option of using TimeBandit instead of VST's internal processing by checking the box in the Edit>Preferences>Audio dialog.

The first step is to divide the audio Part using M Points. Don't Snip them. The M Points are the points which will be pushed or pulled onto the nearest quantize position. Then select Quantize at M-Points from the Do menu. The program will move the Match Points to their closest quantize position and timestretch the audio in between.

This is ideal for tightening-up 'loose' playing such as a slightly out-of-time hi hat line.

Creating Grooves from an audio Part

You know that you can create Grooves from MIDI data. Well, you can also create a Groove from an audio file. The easiest way is to set up M Points in the Audio editor as described above. Then select Match Audio and Tempo from the Do menu. This opens the Audio/Tempo Match editor, Figure 13.22, which shows the M Points below the audio waveform.

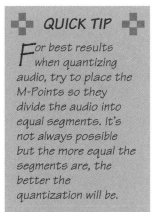

QUICK TIP

For best results when quantizing audio, try to place the M-Points so they divide the audio into equal segments. It's not always possible but the more equal the segments are, the better the quantization will be.

INFO

There's more about quantizing audio and MIDI Parts in Chapter 16.

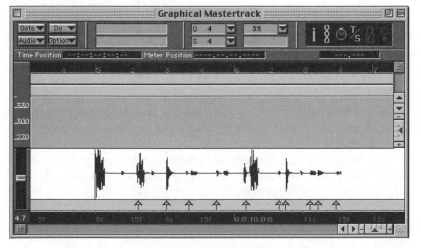

Figure 13.22 The Audio/Tempo Match editor shows M-Points below the audio

This editor also has a Get M-Points function in its Audio menu but if you want to edit the velocities, you have to go back to the Audio editor.

To make a groove, select M-Points to Groove in the Audio menu. VST puts the Groove in the Quantize sub-menu, accessed from the main Functions menu, giving it the name of the audio file. From version 4, VST stores each Groove as a separate file on disk (in the Grooves folder, of course) making it easy to change names and organise the Grooves into any number of sub-folders.

Adding Match Points in the Audio/Tempo editor

The Audio/Tempo editor has no facility for adding extra Match Points. The easiest way to do this is to revert to the Audio editor and add them there.

However, you can add more Match Points in the Audio/Tempo editor simply by duplicating them. Hold down Option on the Mac or Alt on the PC and click and drag a Match Point to a new location. It will click into a position determined by the Snap value (for optimum control you might want to set this to Off).

Finding audio segments

When building up complex arrangements you may find that an audio segment is used many times in a song. You can find out how many times it's used by looking in the Audio Pool. The figure following the speaker icon shows how many times the segment is used, Figure 13.23.

Figure 13.23 The Audio Pool shows how many times a segment is used in a song

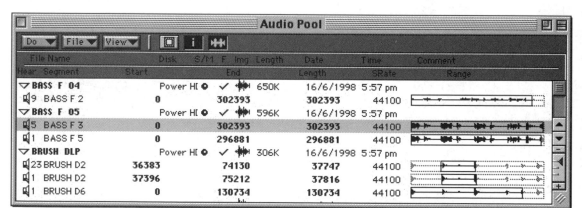

To find out where the segment is used in the song, select it and then select Find Parts in the Do menu. The Parts in the Arrange page will be highlighted.

On the PC, when the Parts have been found and highlighted in the Arrange window, you can select Edit from the Edit menu and open them in the Audio editor.

You can do this, too, on the Mac. However, with the segments selected in the Pool, you can also select Edit from the Edit menu and the segments will each open in the Wave editor.

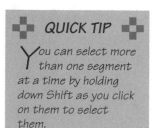

QUICK TIP

You can select more than one segment at a time by holding down Shift as you click on them to select them.

Where's that Part?

The Audio Pool shows which disk the audio segments are stored on. To find out which folder a file is in, on the PC click on the name of the Wave file with the right mouse button, Figure 13.24. On the Mac, hold down the Command key while clicking on the name, Figure 13.25. The PC pop-up also has a Find Target option which opens the folder containing the file.

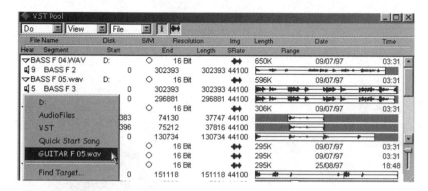

Figure 13.24 Finding where the audio files are on the PC ....

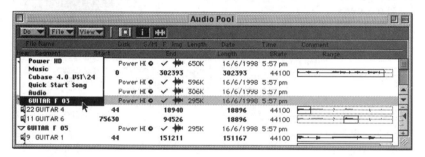

Figure 13.25 ... and the Mac

But if you've been following the advice in this book, all audio files will be in one folder...

Renaming audio files

You can rename audio files on disk, of course, but it's far safer to do it within VST so the program knows about the change of name and doesn't lose track of the file. To rename a file, in the Audio Pool simply double-click on its name, type a new name and press Return.

Duplicating audio files

Before performing a potentially destructive operation on an audio file, it's a good idea to make a copy of it. This is easily done in the Audio Pool. Simply highlight the file, select Duplicate File from the File menu. A file dialog opens prompting you to select a location and a new name for the file.

Replacing a file in the Audio Pool

VST has a good range of effects and processes but there may be times when you want to process a file with an external program. You don't really want to process the original file, and if the file is used in several places in a song, it would be rather time-consuming to replace the original versions with the new versions. The solution is to replace the file in the Audio Pool.

Copy the original file and process it. In the Audio Pool, click in the F column of the file you want to replace (in some versions of VST you may have to click on the Disk column). A pop-up appears asking if you want to re-find the file, Figure 13.26. Click on Yes and navigate to the new file. A dialog will appear warning you that the new file has a different name or date. Click on OK.

Figure 13.26 Replacing a file in the Audio Pool

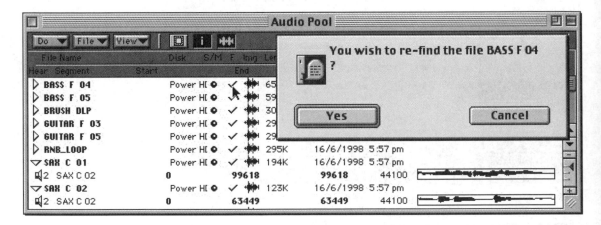

The new file will replace the old one and any segments created from the old file will be taken from the new one. If you want to revert to the original file, just repeat the process.

Note that the new audio must be the same length as the original file for the segment start and end insets to be relevant.

Finding missing files VST can't find

When you open a song, you may get a warning that a file is missing, Figure 13.27. This can happen if it has been moved or renamed since you last saved the song. It can also happen if you have changed its properties such as the date. If you load the song and look in the Audio Pool, the file will appear with three question marks in the Disk column and a crossed circle instead of a tick, Figure 13.28.

During loading, there are options to look for any missing files either manually or automatically. Clicking on the crossed circle also produces these options.

Figure 13.27 VST tells you if it can't find a file

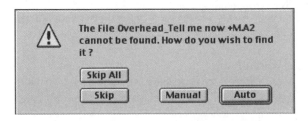

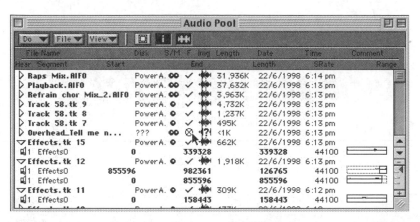

Figure 13.28 Missing files are indicated by a crossed circle in the Audio Pool

The Auto function scans all your hard disks. Sometimes, however, it may still not find a missing file. In most cases this is because the file has been renamed or its creation date has been changed. VST is quite strict about this. If you have used a program which has changed the creation date, say by processing it in a wave editor, then VST may not be able to find it. You can then elect to find it manually.

When you find the file, the program will warn you that the name and/or date is not the same but it will let you proceed anyway. The next time you open the song, the program will look for the file at that location.

Deleting unwanted files and backing-up

VST has several functions for removing and deleting unwanted audio files – Purge Segments, Erase Unused and Prepare Archive, all available from the Audio Pool. These are great ways to remove unwanted and unused files and free-up hard disk space.

But do be aware of Murphy's Law. If you delete files before backing them up while working on a song you can bet your bottom rupee that you'll need them before the song is complete.

So the first rule of file deletion is – don't! Not until the song is in the can and you're sure you won't need the files for a remix. With today's low-cost back-up media such as CDs, you should never have to delete a file simply to free-up disk space.

When a song is complete, it is a good idea to run the Prepare Master function from the Audio Pool's File menu. It combines the functions of Purge Segments, Erase Unused and Prepare Archive. It extracts only the bits of the audio files actually used in the song and stores them in new files, and it updates the song to play the new files.

It prompts for a new folder and stores the files in it, ready for backing up. The routine will warn you if you select a disk which does not have enough space for all the files. It's a good idea to save the song itself into that folder. Check that it plays okay (you never know!) and then backup the entire archive.

QUICK TIP

If you know where a file is and have a lot of hard disk real estate, it's quicker to find it manually than to use the Auto function which scans your entire hard disk system.

INFO

There's more about using Prepare Archive and backing up in Chapter 17.

Audio and MIDI effects

VST's effects
In order to use VST's effects, er, effectively, it's necessary to know how they fit into the signal chain. Experienced users may wish to skip this section.

VST has three types of effect – Send, Insert and Master.

Send effects.
These are probably the most commonly-used effects and the system works very much like a 'real' mixer. These effects are selected in the Audio Send Effects rack, Figure 14.1, and the new racks in VST v4 can hold up to eight effects. The effects in the rack are global in the sense that they can be accessed by any audio channel.

Figure 14.1 The Audio Send Effects rack

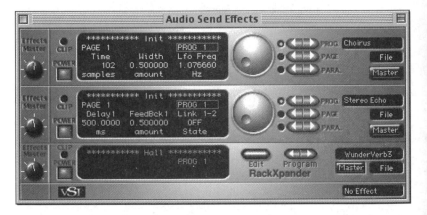

To route a Track to the effects rack you must open its EQ window which you can do in two ways. You can select the Track and click on the FX/EQ button in the Inspector, or you can open the Audio Channel Mixer and click on the Track's FX/EQ button there, Figure 14.2.

The effects section is housed between the fader and the EQ section. There are eight little sections here, one for each of the effects, and you route a Track to an effect by clicking the On button in the section of the effect you want to use, Figure 14.3. The dial controls the amount of signal sent to the effect – the Send level or volume.

You can, therefore, route a single audio channel to up to eight effects and you can route any number of audio channels through a single effect.

Figure 14.2 (left) Click on the FX/EQ button to open the effects rack

Figure 14.3 (right) Switch an effect on with its on button!

That's in theory, of course. The actual number you will be able to achieve depends on several factors, not least of all the power of your computer.

The output from the effects rack is routed either to the Master output or to one of the Group buses (there are eight of these), selected from a drop-down menu at the bottom of each channel, Figure 14.4, where it can be mixed with the dry signal if required.

These effects are mono in, stereo out.

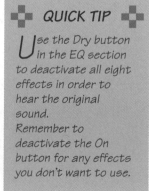

QUICK TIP

Use the Dry button in the EQ section to deactivate all eight effects in order to hear the original sound.
Remember to deactivate the On button for any effects you don't want to use.

Figure 14.4 The output is selected from a drop-down menu

Insert effects.

These effects are inserted directly into the signal chain of an audio channel. The effects are accessed by clicking on the Insert button in the Audio Channel Mixer, Figure 14.5, which opens the Insert effects rack. Each audio channel has its own Insert rack which can hold four effects. Each channel can use a different set of effects in its Insert rack.

Figure 14.5 The Insert button opens the Insert Effects rack

INFO

A dry or direct signal is an unprocessed signal, usually the original signal. A wet signal is the processed signal. With certain types of effect such as reverb and chorus it's usual to mix the two in a wet/dry mix to achieve the desired result.

With an Insert effect, the entire signal is routed through the effect – you can't perform a wet/dry mix. It is, therefore, best suited to effects which change the entire sound such as compression, distortion and EQ.

Insert effects are serial, that is the signal is passed through the effects from the top one downwards.

Master effects.

These effects are applied to the entire stereo output via the Master bus. The rack can be opened by clicking on the Master FX button at the top of the Master Mixer, Figure 14.6. This rack can also hold four effects and there is no mixing of wet and dry signals. In other words, the effects here are applied to the entire stereo output. Like the Insert rack, suitable effects include filters, dynamics processing and so on.

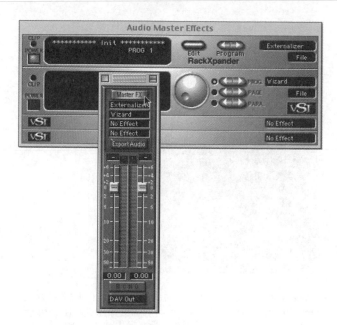

Figure 14.6 The Master FX
button opens the Master FX
rack – which is the way it
should be

Only effects with a stereo input can be used as a Master effect, whether or not the Mono button at the bottom of the Master Mixer is activated. Some plug-in effects come in both mono and stereo versions and VST includes some effects suitable for use on the Master bus such as the Externalizer and Scopion, Figure 14.7.

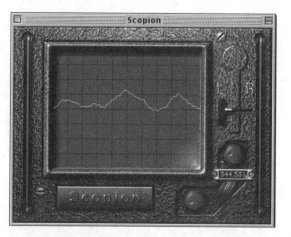

Figure 14.7 Scopion has a
stereo input and is suitable
for use in the Master FX rack

Pre and Post Send

The effects section of a Track's EQ window, Figure 14.8, includes a Pre button. This switches between Pre and Post fader send. With Pre send (the button selected), the total volume level of the signal is sent to the effects rack.

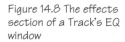
Figure 14.8 The effects
section of a Track's EQ
window

With Post fader send (the Pre button not selected), the amount of the signal sent to the effects rack is controlled by the fader.

When do you use what? In most instances you will use Post send and if in doubt, try this first. However, Pre send can be used to send a good level of signal to the effects if the volume level of the Track is set low. With Pre fader you can change the level of the signal in a mix without reducing the amount of signal sent to the effect. As an example, use this with reverb and fade the main signal and it will sound as though it is vanishing into the distance.

Send and Return levels

There is always a temptation to whack the Send and Return levels of the Send effects up full and leave them there. The issue is further complicated because some effects have input and output level controls, all of which has a bearing on the volume levels floating around the system.

As a rule of thumb, set the levels to around 80 percent of full and tweak from there. Keep your eye on the Clip indicator just above the On button in the Send Effects rack. If it's clipping, reduce the level.

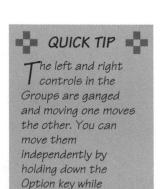

QUICK TIP

The left and right controls in the Groups are ganged and moving one moves the other. You can move them independently by holding down the Option key while dragging with the mouse.

Using the Audio Group Mixer

VST has eight Audio Group Mixers, Figure 14.9, each consisting of a stereo channel pair. They have their own window and can be opened from the Panel menu. They also appear in the Audio Channel Mixer if you scroll the window to the right.

You can route an effect send to a Group. In the Track's EQ window, select the required Group from the Send Routing pop-up menu, Figure 14.10. Note that the routing is to one side of the Group's stereo pair. Each of the Groups has its own Insert effect so with this method you can route several effect Sends to the same Group and process them with the same effect and effect settings.

Figure 14.9 There are eight Audio Group Mixers

Figure 14.10 You can route an effects send to a group via a pop-up menu

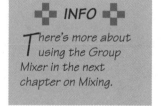

INFO

There's more about using the Group Mixer in the next chapter on Mixing.

How to use more effects than your computer can handle

VST's virtual effects are great but they do require a fair amount of processing power. Some effects are very CPU-intensive and seem to hog the entire machine. The effects supplied with VST have a very low CPU requirement (the Grungelizer makes the heaviest demands) and not all third-party plug-ins tell you their CPU load. You can get an approximate idea by activating the Audio Performance Meter, Figure 14.11, while running the effects.

If you want to use CPU-intensive effects or if your computer is not up to running the number of effects you require, you can mix down the audio, incorporating the effects into the mix.

To do this, set the left and right Locators to encompass the section of audio you want to process and select Export Audio Tracks from the File

Figure 14.11 The Audio Performance Meter tells you how much more your system can take without falling over

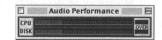

menu. The dialog box, Figure 14.12, gives you the option of including Effects and Master Effects as well as Automation. As this is done off-line, any number of heavily processor-intensive effects can be used.

The resulting file which is saved to disk can then be imported back into the arrangement and you can carry on creating your song.

Figure 14.12 The Export Audio Tracks dialog box

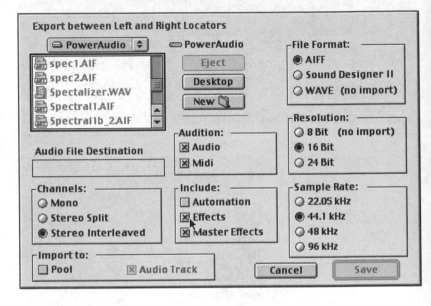

Free effects!

Yes, that's right! The VST and the DirectX plug-in formats are the most popular digital audio plug-in formats so far devised, and dozens of programmers have created effects which they give away absolutely free. Even more are available for a small registration charge. Even commercial developers give away free plug-ins.

These are all readily available on the Internet. A good way to find them is to do a search on 'VST' and 'plug-ins'. A good place to start is the KnowledgeBase at the Steinberg Web site. This and other useful Web site URLs are in Appendix 3, page 151 (URL – Uniform Resource Locator, the unique address which can point to a Web site or even to a page on a Web site.)

The KnowledgeBase plug-ins section includes the URLs of developers of free software. But keeping up to date is not easy and the site may not have details of 'every' free plug-in. Most developer's sites include links to other plug-in sites so do check them all out.

Filter sweep effects

Some plug-ins allow you to create filter sweeps and other dynamic effects – the built-in AutoPan effect is one such example. However, you can also create these and other dynamic effects using VST's mixer automation features. There's more about this in the next Chapter.

EQ tips

There are probably more tips on using EQ than all other aspects of music put together! So as not to let the side down, here are a few more, most of which you have probably already heard:

- Don't try to fix it in the mix. Yes, this old chestnut. It's far better to make a good recording in the first place – a recording which you have tried to tart up with a spot of EQ is unlikely to sound as good.
- Having said that, if you can't do a retake, you may have little option but to try to fix it in the mix... But make it a necessity rather than an excuse for not paying much attention to the recording in the first place.
- As a general rule, try to cut rather than boost. Boosting increases noise as well as signal.
- If you do boost, always check the overall output level. Boosting generally increases the level of specific frequencies which could cause clipping.
- To EQ a bass guitar use 2 – 4kHz for its mid range and 80 – 120Hz for the lower end.
- To make a section stand out, boost the 1 – 5kHz range (this is the range speech falls into) but don't boost this region of all the parts.
- Ignore all these tips and let your ears be your guide.

> **INFO**
>
> *The Hi Quality button in the EQ section gives the EQ bands a +/–24db range as opposed to a +/–12dB range and generally offers better quality. It should be used by choice although it does require more CPU power.*

Virtual vector synthesis

In the mid-90s there was a lot of interest in dynamically-changing sounds, and a few synthesisers featured a process called vector synthesis. It's rather like morphing. One sound is gradually changed or blended into another, either by twiddling a joystick or by programming. You can create a virtual morph between any two sounds by fading one in while fading the other one out.

Create a MIDI part. Copy it to another Track on another MIDI channel and assign the two Tracks or Parts different sounds. Now create an empty Part. Draw a volume curve increasing from 0 to 127 or use whatever volume range you want the sound to play through. A range of 15 to

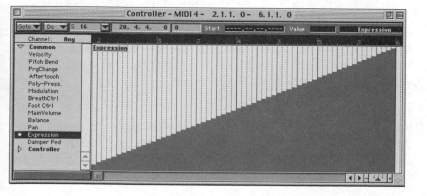

Figure 14.13 Drawing a fade in the Controller editor

120 may be more suitable. You can use Main Volume, Expression or even Velocity but see Chapter 4 for a discussion of the pros and cons of using these for making volume changes. It's easy to draw in curves using the Controller editor, Figure 14.13, but you can also use the Controller area of the Key editor.

Copy the Part to another Track and open it in the Key editor. Select Reverse from the Do menu and the fade will be reversed, Figure 14.14.

Figure 14.14 Reversing the fade

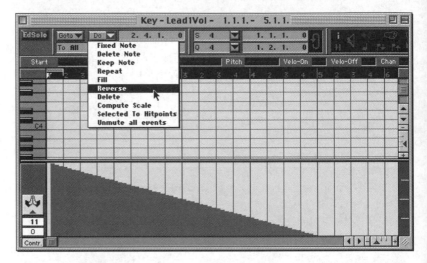

Figure 14.15 The fades are assigned to respective MIDI Parts

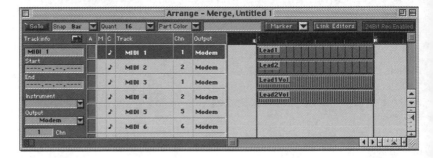

Assign the two fade Parts to the same MIDI channels as the two MIDI Parts, Figure 14.15. During playback, the first Part will fade in while the other fades out creating a morphing effect. You may need to fiddle with the relative volumes of the two Parts to get the best effect which is why it may not be best not to use Volume for the fade. This can be particularly effective when used with long notes and sustaining sounds although this won't work if you use Velocity for the curve!

Sisters of morphy

You can use the above principle to create more complex morphs using three, four or more sounds. You could have each of the sounds fading in and out in turn, or you could have two sounds fading in while one was fading out. There are many combinations.

Open the gate

As well as drawing Volume curves into an editor, you can also draw in Volume spikes to create gate effects.

You can create all sorts of effects like this from regular on/off gates to echo-type gates and gates with distinctive rhythms. Keyfax Software's Twiddly Bits Volume 2 (see Appendix 3 page 151) contains a collection of gate effects.

Using Logical edit you can easily assign an individual Volume level to each note but you can also create rhythmic gate effects which you can apply to any music line – a lead line with lots of notes, a strumming guitar riff or a sustained pad.

Figure 14.16 shows a very regular gate rhythm which has very small periods of silence in between the Ons. Figure 14.17 is still a regular pattern but the sound never actually hits zero volume. Figure 14.18 is more complex and alternates a full volume level with a series of levels which increase in volume.

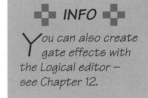

INFO

You can also create gate effects with the Logical editor – see Chapter 12.

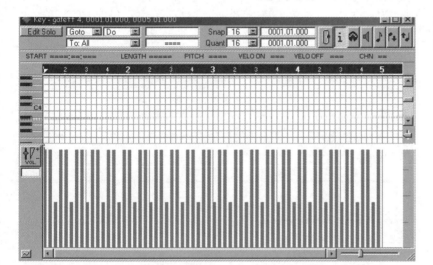

Figure 14.16 A regular gate pattern with silence between the Ons

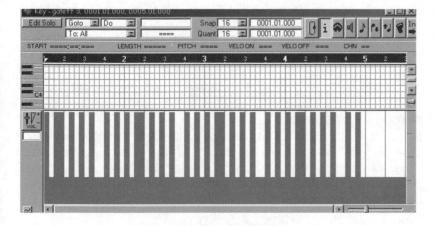

Figure 14.17 This gate pattern never hits zero volume

Figure 14.18 A more complex gate pattern

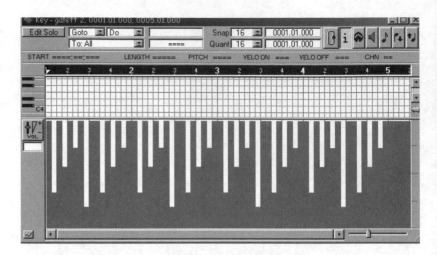

Gate effects with audio Parts

You can also create gate effects with audio Parts using dynamic events by drawing the gate directly below the audio in the Audio editor, Figure 14.19. See Chapter 13 for more about dynamic events.

Figure 14.19 Drawing gate effects into the Audio editor

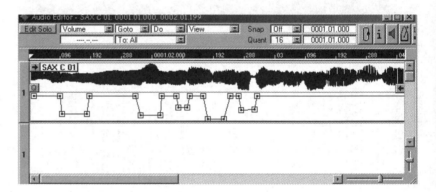

Alternatively, if you know the rhythm of the gate effect you want to create, you can cut the audio at strategic points, say every 1/16th or 1/8th beat, and then set each segment to the required volume level. In many ways this is the easier option as you don't have to fiddle with the breakpoints but do remember to backup the song or audio file before you start.

And remember, you can use dynamic events to create pan effects, too.

Real-time XG/GS modulations

If you have an XG or GS instrument you'll know that many of their parameters such as resonance and filter cutoff can be altered in real-time. You just need to ply it with the right Controller data. Some keyboards can generate any type of Controller but if yours doesn't you can still tweak the settings by remapping.

From the Options menu, open the MIDI System Setup dialog, Figure 14.20. In the Controller Map section, select a Controller. This might be the Modulation wheel or Data Entry slider. In the Mapped section select the Controller you want use. For XG and GS instruments these will probably be Controllers 70 to 74. Check the specs of your instrument to see what it supports.

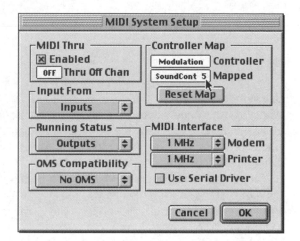

Figure 14.20 The MIDI System Setup dialog

The data is mapped in real-time and you can record it, too, so you can create real-time filter sweeps, for example, and make real-time changes to other parameters.

15

Mixing it

❖ INFO ❖

There's more about Window Sets in Chapter 3.

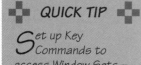

❖ QUICK TIP ❖

Set up Key Commands to access Window Sets – it's faster than selecting them from the Windows menu.

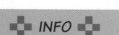

❖ INFO ❖

There's more about using the Group Mixer in the previous chapter.

Use Window Sets

With VST v4, Window Sets were added to the program. These allow you to save the entire layout of the screen – including the effects and mixers whose positions were not remembered in earlier versions of VST (which didn't have Window Sets anyway).

They are particularly useful when mixing because the mixer and effects can easily fill the entire screen so you can create Window Sets to flip back and forth between mixer and effects, the Arrange page and any other windows that you wish.

Use a high screen resolution

Mixing is one aspect of computer-based music making which really benefits from a lot of screen real-estate. You can probably get by with a resolution of 800 x 600 but 1024 x 768 is preferable. A higher resolution is even better but may require a larger monitor. If you're a regular VST user and particularly if you do a lot of mixing, it's well worth considering a 21 inch monitor. You'll wonder how on earth you managed before.

Figure 15.1 shows VST laid out on a 1900 x 1200 screen. We had to severely reduce it to fit it onto these pages so it looks a bit like a printed circuit board, but you can see a full 26-channel Audio mixer plus the eight stereo paired channels of the Group mixer followed by the Master mixer along the bottom. There's plenty of room for an effects rack or two, a few effects open for editing and lots of room to still be able to see the Arrange page clearly. Now that's mixing!

Two monitors

Windows 98 and the Mac Operating System support the use of two monitors. Even a spare, small monitor could be pressed into use to give you more screen space. Depending on its resolution you could either dedicate it to the mixer windows or to the Arrange page.

Using the Group mixer

VST has eight Group mixers (stereo channel pairs) which you'll find on the Audio Channel Mixer if you scroll far enough to the right. It can also be opened in its own window.

The Group mixer has several useful functions in VST. For example, it makes it easy to process several audio Tracks with the same settings

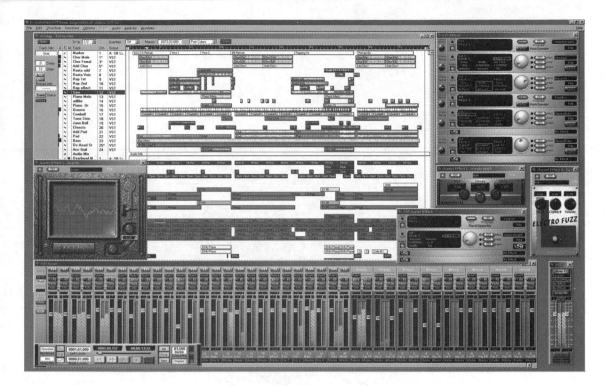

Figure 15.1 VST operating at a very nice resolution of 1900 x 1200

simultaneously. At the bottom of each audio channel is a drop-down menu where you determine its output, Figure 15.2. You can, therefore, route any number of the audio channels to a single Group. They can then all be controlled by one pair of faders, mute and solo buttons.

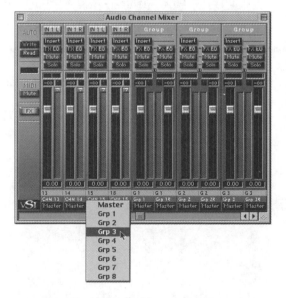

Figure 15.2 You can route an audio channel to any of the groups

What's more, they can all be routed through the same effects as each Group channel has its own Insert effect. Not only does this ensure that each channel is processed in exactly the same way, it puts far less demand on the CPU than running several channels through their own effects. Use Group channels with effects such as reverb and EQ.

Furthermore, you can route Group channels to other Group channels! You might think you'd get your routings tied up in knots but the system is very easy to follow because it only allows a Group to be routed to a higher-numbered Group. Figure 15.3 is a composite illustration showing how it works.

Figure 15.3 Groups can only be routed to a higher-numbered group

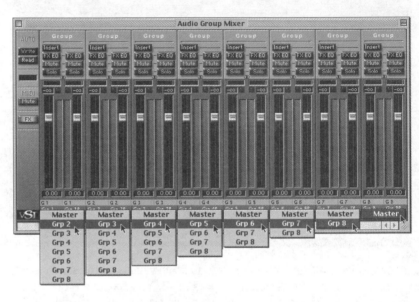

Mixer automation

To record real-time changes you make in the mixer into the song, you activate the Write button in the mixer. This creates a special Audio Mix Track where the automation data is stored. You do not have to be in normal Record mode to do this; the automation is written during play mode. To activate the automation, select the Read button in the mixer.

Virtually every function in VST can be automated. Here's a list.

For each channel and Group
- Volume
- Pan
- Mute
- Solo
- EQ On button
- Settings for 4 EQ modules
- 8 x Effect Send Active switches
- 8 x Effect Send levels
- 8 x Effect Send Pre switches
- Effect Dry switch
- 4 x Insert Effect program selection (audio channels 1 – 32 only)
- 4 x Insert Effect Parameters (the first 15 for each effect, audio channels 1 – 32 only)

For all channels
- Master volume left and right
- 8 x Send effect Master level
- 8 x Send effect program selection
- 8 x Send effect parameters (the first 16 for each effect)
- 4 x Master effect program selection
- 4 x Master effect parameters (the first 8 for each effect)

Useful mixer keystrokes

One function which you will invariably want to do time and time again is to reset mixer controls to their centre or default position. Other useful functions include the ability to move faders in a stereo pair independently. Here are the keys which do it:

Mixer keystrokes

Mac	PC	Mouse	Action
		Click on clip indicator	Resets it
Command	Ctrl	Click on fader	Reset to 0dB
Command	Ctrl	Click on pan	Reset to centre
Command	Ctrl	Click on EQ button	Toggle EQ on and off (EQ must have been enabled in EQ window)
Command	Ctrl	Click on FX button	Toggles between Dry and all enabled FX Sends on and off
Option	Alt	Move fader, solo, mute in stereo pair	Moves one side of the pair independently
Option	Alt	Move control in a mono channel	Also moves the controls in adjacent channel

Optimising automation

Automation is one of the great things about the VST mixer. However, you may have noticed that it stores all its automation data on one Track which can make individual channels difficult to edit.

The easiest way around this is to record automation for one channel at a time and move each Audio Mix recording onto a new Track.

Record your automations for the first channel, deactivate Write, go to the Arrange page, create a new Mixer Track and drag the Audio Mix Part onto it. It's probably a good idea to name the Track – something like 'Chan1Mix' sounds good. Record the automation for the second channel. The automation data will be written to the original Audio Mix Track. Create another Mixer Track and repeat as before.

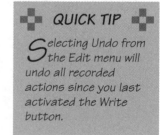

✚ QUICK TIP ✚

Selecting Undo from the Edit menu will undo all recorded actions since you last activated the Write button.

Editing automation data

The Audio Mix Track can be opened in the Controller editor by double-clicking on it in the Arrange page and the events edited therein, Figure 15.4. A dot next to a parameter indicates that data has been recorded for it.

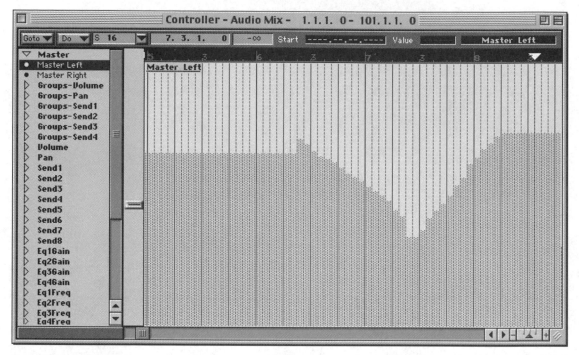

Figure 15.4 You can edit the Audio Mix Track in the Controller editor

✚ INFO ✚

In Figure 15.4, all volume and pan parameters are marked with a dot because the first time you activate the Write function in the mixer, the current values are written at the beginning of the Track.

You can draw in fader curves and the like although to some this may seem to defeat the object of using mixer automation in the first place. But if there's a blip in the data or if you missed a cue, it's often easier to edit a small piece of data than to record the whole thing again.

You can also open the Audio Mix data in the List editor, Figure 15.5. Parameters with on/off values such as the Mute buttons can only be edited here, not in the Controller editor.

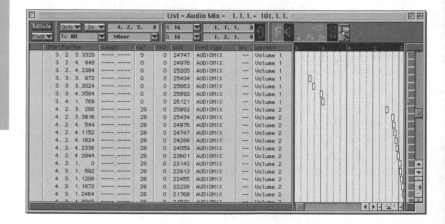

Figure 15.5 Audio mix data can be edited in the List editor

Alternative volume and pan automation

If you have an audio Part containing sections at different volume levels which you need to balance or with pan settings you want to create, instead of using mixer automation use dynamic events. This is often a much easier way to create fades than to try to do it manually. Chapter 13 explains how to do this.

If you simply want to set different sections of a recording to different volume levels rather than create dynamic changes, select the Scissors Tool and cut the Part into segments. Select the Pencil and drag the volume lines of the segments to the required levels, Figure 15.6.

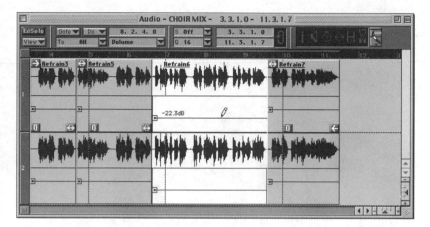

Figure 15.6 An easy way to set sections of audio to different volume levels

Creating filter sweeps and other dynamic effects

Check back at the list of functions which VST's automation supports and you'll see that it includes effects. Yes, that means you can tweak effect parameters in real-time creating dynamic changes to the sound.

The process is exactly the same as creating volume and pan automation except you change the parameters of the effects in the Effects rack. You can also twiddle the dials in a Track's EQ section creating filter sweeps.

You can automate the parameters of many third-party plug-in effects, too (although not all support automation). A particular favourite is Arboretum's Hyperprism which was designed specifically to be 'played with' in real-time. In the stand-alone version, you drag the mouse around the infamous Blue Window, Figure 15.7 which modifies assignable parameters, changing the sound in real-time as you do so.

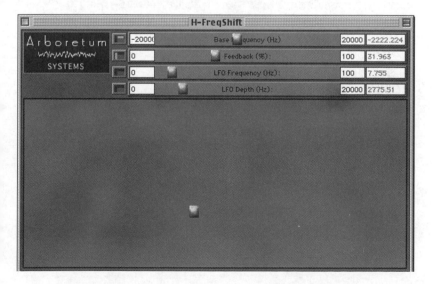

Figure 15.7 Arboretum's Hyperprism was made to be played

The VST plug-in version contains 35 effects and although you can set up static parameters and use them like 'normal' effects, they really come into their own when manipulated in real-time. And VST's automation facilities allow you to do this.

MIDI mixing

VST v4 introduced the MIDI Track Mixer, Figure 15.8. It automatically expands and contracts, adding and removing channels whenever you add or delete a Track and it can expand up to 128 Tracks – try fitting those onto a 14 inch monitor!

Figure 15.8 The MIDI Track Mixer

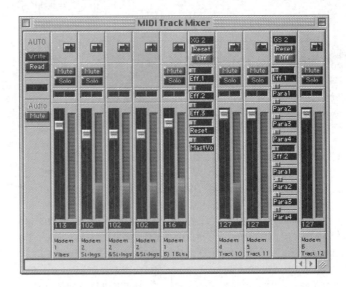

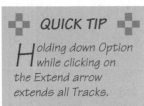

QUICK TIP

Holding down Option while clicking on the Extend arrow extends all Tracks.

Modelled on the VST audio mixer, the MIDI mixer has similar fader, pan, mute and solo controls plus automation facilities. You can, therefore, perform real-time MIDI mixing and automation in the same way as audio mixing. Again, however, you may be able to create some functions such as fades more easily manually in the Controller editor or using the Logical editor.

However, each channel can be 'extended' to show another channel strip which can be loaded with different modules offering a range of additional functions, Figure 15.9.

Figure 15.9 You can load a range of modules into the MIDI Mixer

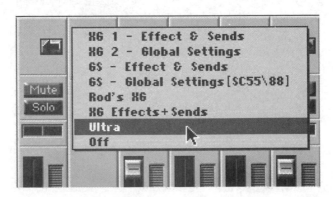

VST comes with XG and GS modules for setting up global parameters such as the type of reverb and chorus used, and for adjusting effect parameters such as the send levels for these effects. And yes, you can use these to make real-time effects changes.

As an example, the XG1 Effects & Sends module, Figure 15.10, contains the following parameters:

Send 1	Send level for reverb
Send 2	Send level for chorus
Send 3	Send level for the Variation effect
Attack	Attack time
Release	Release time
Harm. C	Harmonic content
Bright	Brightness

INFO

XG *is Yamaha's extended version of the General MIDI format, GS is Roland's version.*

Figure 15.10 One of the XG Modules

Adjusting the Harmonic Content or the Brightness in real-time will create tonal sweeps. The GS Effects & Sends module has even more parameters including Cutoff and Resonance controls.

Mixing and mastering

The ultimate destination of a song is most likely to be a final stereo recording which can be used for mastering. There are several ways to create this file.

Most users will want to record to DAT (or perhaps to a cassette) or burn the audio to CD.

To record to an external unit such as a DAT, you simply route the audio and MIDI outputs to the DAT. If you are using a sound card for both audio and MIDI, you will be able to connect the card's audio output directly to the DAT. If the card has a digital connection, so much the better, as you'll be able to record to DAT with no loss of quality.

If you are using external MIDI equipment, you need to bring both audio and MIDI data together and the easiest way to do this is with a mixer. You then connect the mixer's output to the DAT. If you have more than one piece of outboard equipment you ought to have a mixer. However, there is another way as we'll see in a moment.

These methods require the recording to be done in real-time. In other words, VST must be capable of playing back all the audio and MIDI data, complete with any effects you may have used, without glitching. If it can, fine. If it sometimes stumbles, you may want to consider mixing down to a stereo file – coming right up in the next section.

Once the song has been recorded to DAT it can be sent off for mastering or, if you want to burn your own CD, it can be recorded back into VST as a stereo audio file.

Mixing down audio Tracks

If you want to burn your material to CD, you need to mix it down to a stereo audio file and save it to a hard disk because that's the format CD burning software requires. If your song has so many parts or requires more processing power than your computer can comfortably handle, you can circumvent the stuttering, glitching and dropouts by mixing it down to a stereo file.

Mixing down in VST is very easy and has been touched on in Chapter 14. You use the Export Audio Tracks function in the File menu. Set the Left and Right Locators to the start and end of the song (or the section you want to mix down) and set up the Tracks, effects and automation so it all plays as required.

It doesn't matter at this stage if playback stutters because you're running too many effects or your hard disk is too slow, because the mixdown processes the files off-line and speed is not critical.

Now select the Export Audio File option. The resulting dialog, Figure 15.11, has several options which enable you to select the file format and so on that you want to use. Of prime interest is the Include section which allows you to include automation and effects in the mixdown.

The resulting file can then be used with suitable CD-R software to create a track on an audio CD.

Figure 15.11 When mixing down audio files you can include automation and effects even if your computer cannot handle them in real-time

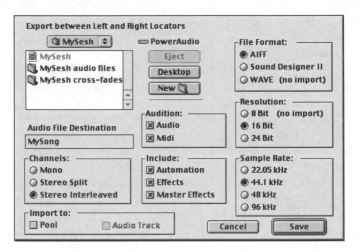

Mixing down audio and MIDI Tracks

In order to include MIDI Tracks in a mixdown to hard disk, they must first be converted to digital audio. You can do this by recording everything to DAT first as described above and then recording the DAT to a VST audio Track. Alternatively, you can record the MIDI Tracks into VST as audio.

To do this, route the MIDI output to the input you use for recording into VST. The output will most likely come from a mixer or a sound card or it might come direct from a sound module or synthesiser. Some sound cards have an option to record internally and can route the MIDI output to the recording input which is neat. Otherwise connect the card's audio Out to its audio In and proceed as if you were recording an audio Track in VST. Make sure that the audio Tracks in the song are muted and disable any other input which may be a source of noise.

Once the MIDI Tracks have been recorded, mute the real MIDI Tracks, unmute the audio Tracks and export the whole song as an audio file as before.

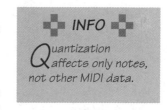

16

Quantization and Grooves

Types of quantization

VST has a wealth of quantize options, Figure 16.1, which all work in slightly different ways. Here's what they do.

Over Quantize

This is Cubase's version of the 'standard' quantize function which pushes and pulls notes onto the nearest division of the beat. However, it also analyses the recorded performance and detects chords, even if the notes are slightly ahead of or behind the beat, and it holds the notes in the chord together during quantization.

✣ **INFO** ✣

Quantization affects only notes, not other MIDI data.

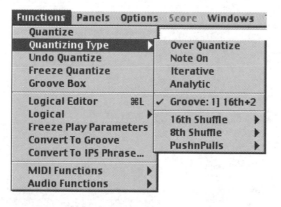

Figure 16.1 VST's quantize options

Iterative Quantize

This is useful for tidying up a recording without slamming all the notes squarely onto a specified beat division. In other sequencers it's known as partial quantize. It has two parameters which you set up in the Preferences>MIDI>Quantize dialog, Figure 16.2. The Strength Percentage

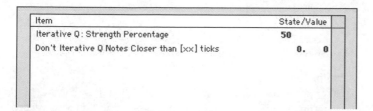

Figure 16.2 Setting up Iterative Quantize

is the amount by which the notes are moved towards the quantize value. A setting of 50 percent means they are moved only half way. This tidies up the timing but retains some of the inaccuracies which we attribute to 'human feel'.

The 'Don't Iterative Q Notes Closer than' parameter lets you specify a value in 1/16th notes and ticks and any notes closer than this setting will not be moved. So if you think any notes within 300 ticks of the beat are close enough for jazz, it prevents the function from moving them. If you want to apply some quantization but retain some feel, use this.

Note On Quantize
This moves the note start positions just like Over Quantize but it doesn't move the end positions. As a result the lengths of the notes will change.

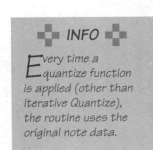

Analytic Quantize
This one's a bit clever. It's designed for use with music which contains a mix of straight notes and triplets. It doesn't quantize notes which are too far away from the quantize value. Trying to analyse and quantize a mix of straight notes and triplets is a devil of job. Often the only way to do it is to quantize a section at a time. But before you do, give this a shot.

Match Quantize
This is a special quantize function activated with the Match Quantize Tool. It is used to impose the feel of one Part onto another. Common uses would be to impose the feel of a bass drum line on a hi hat line or a bass guitar line on a drum part. You can use this to match audio and MIDI parts and there's more about doing so in Chapter 5.

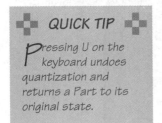

Groove Quantize
This is another special type of quantization designed not to correct timing errors but to change the feel of a part. VST comes with lots of Grooves which appear in the Quantizing Type menu, Figure 16.3. You can load new Grooves and create your own.

Figure 16.3 Grooves appear off the Quantizing Type menu

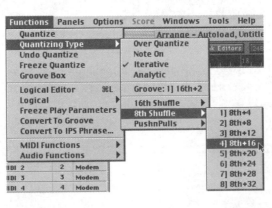

Auto quantization
Switching on the AQ button in the Transport Bar, Figure 16.4, activates Automatic Quantization which quantizes everything you record according

to the current Quantize Type. This can be a good shortcut if you know that what you're recording will respond well to a particular type of quantization. To retain the maximum amount of human feel, however, you may prefer to record straight and only quantize those sections which need it.

Figure 16.4 Activating Automatic Quantization

Undoing quantization

Quantization is always undoable, even after you've saved a file to disk. The original data is always preserved until you Freeze it.

Freeze Quantize

Freeze Quantize, available from the Functions menu, permanently fixes the current quantization setting. This should be used when you are 110 percent sure that the Part is exactly how you want it. Because each quantize uses the original notes, Freeze can also be useful if you want to quantize in several steps in which case you'd Freeze after each one. But do backup your data before using it. Freezing cannot be undone.

Using the Groove Tool

The Groove Tool, Figure 16.5 (right), was introduced with VST v4 and is a great time-saver. Select it, click on a Part and a pop-up box appears, similar to the bottom of the Quantizing Type menu, where you can select a Groove and apply it to the part, Figure 16.6.

You can apply it to several parts at once by selecting them first but you must also check the 'Tools work on All Selected Parts' box in the Preferences>General>Arrangement dialog, Figure 16.7.

Figure 16.5 The Groove Tool

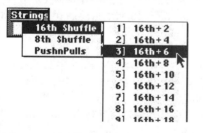

Using the Groove Box

Creating your own Grooves is not something everyone can easily do but the Groove Box, introduced with VST v4, makes it very easy.

Select the Part you want to quantize and set it up to cycle during playback. Select a quantize value which will be the maximum amount a note can be moved to fit a Groove. 1/16th and 1/8th notes are good starting points but it depends on the notes and the results you want to obtain. You can change this later at any time.

Select the Groove Box, Figure 16.8, from the Functions menu. The display shows the Grooves and Groove folders on your disk. Select one to try

Figure 16.6 (left) Select a Groove with the Groove Tool

Figure 16.7 (right) Checking this lets you apply a groove to all selected parts

Figure 16.8 The Groove Box
makes Groove-making easy

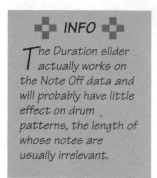

> **+ INFO +**
>
> *The Duration slider actually works on the Note Off data and will probably have little effect on drum patterns, the length of whose notes are usually irrelevant.*

> **+ INFO +**
>
> *Grooves are stored as files in the Groove folder – of course – on your hard disk.*

Figure 16.9 The Match
Quantize Tool

> **+ INFO +**
>
> *You can turn a MIDI Part into a Groove by highlighting it and selecting Convert to Groove from the Functions menu. It will be saved as a file to disk and entered in the lower part of the Groove menu.*

and check the Prelisten box so you can hear the results in real-time.

Then mess with the sliders. The Timing, Velocity and Duration sliders all determine how much of the relevant aspect of a Groove is applied to the pattern. Note that not all Grooves include velocity information.

When you're happy with the result, click on the Do it button to quantize the data. The settings of the sliders are retained when you close the Box and will be used the next time you use Groove Quantize even if it's not via the Groove Box.

Quantizing MIDI to audio Parts

An easy way to apply the feel of an audio Part to a MIDI Part is to select the Match Quantize Tool, Figure 16.9, pick up the audio Part and drag it on top of the MIDI Part. First, however, you need to create Match Points for the audio Part...

This can be easily done although it's easier with some types of audio Part than others. Double-click on the audio Part to open the Audio edit window. In the View menu, make sure Dynamic Events is selected. In the data type menu, select M-Points (the other two options are Volume and Pan), Figure 16.10.

Set a suitable Snap value. Like Snap in the other editors, this determines where Match Points can be placed. It's usually best to turn this off completely but you may need to experiment.

Select the audio Part and then select Get M-Points from the Do menu.

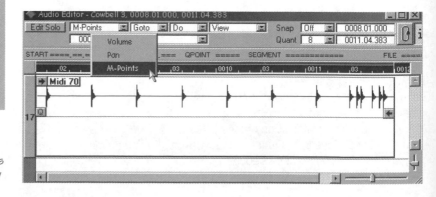

Figure 16.10 Select M-Points
so they appear in the display

A pop-up box asks questions about Sensitivity, Attack and so on, Figure 16.11. The default settings are worth going with. You can change them later if they don't work very well (and you might like to read the manual for more information about them before you do so). Click on the Process button and Match Points will appear below the audio, Figure 16.12.

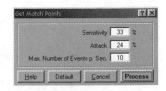

Figure 16.11 How sensitive are your M-Points?

The Match Points correspond to the volume levels in the audio file and they occur at peaks. This is readily seen in a drum or percussion part. The black squares at the top of the Points represent velocity levels. Both these and the positions of Match Points can be changed by clicking and dragging

Figure 16.12 Fitting Match Points to audio

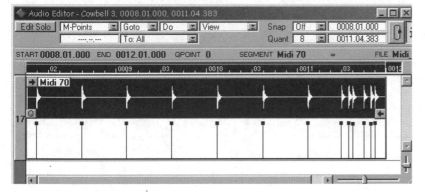

with the Pencil Tool. You can add Match Points manually by clicking with the Pencil Tool while holding down Alt on the PC or Option on the Mac.

Now, when you drag the audio Part onto a MIDI Part with the Match Quantize Tool, a dialog will appear asking if you want to include accents which are the velocity values of the Match Points. The quantize settings in the audio file will then be applied to the MIDI file.

Quantizing audio to MIDI Parts

This is slightly more tricky and if you think about how quantization works, you'll realise why. When you quantize a MIDI part, you push and pull notes onto specific divisions of the beat. As an audio file is one long continuous event, in order to quantize it we need to split it up into several individual events. That's essentially what Steinberg's ReCycle does and if you've used that you'll be way ahead of us here. But even if you don't have ReCycle, you can still split up audio events and quantize them in VST.

The first step is to divide the audio Part into quantizable events which you do with Match Points as described above, Figure 16.13. Select the Part then select Snip at M-Points from the Do menu. The Part will split into segments, Figure 16.14.

Now with the Match Quantize Tool, drag the MIDI Part onto the audio Part. A dialog will appear asking if you want to use Dynamic Time Compression. Click on No and the start positions of the audio Part will be quantized to the events in the MIDI Part.

You need to be aware that this system does have its limitations. If the quantize process increases the gaps between the audio parts by too much there will be gaps between audio events. ReCycle has a Stretch function which extends the release portion of a segment to fill in such gaps.

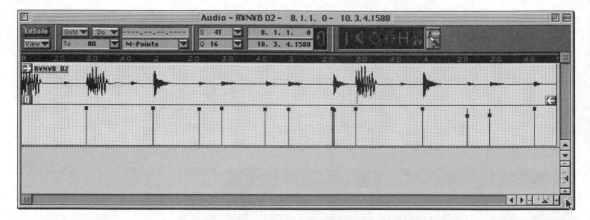

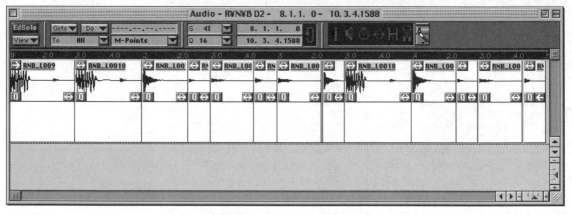

Figure 16.13 (top) Adding Match Points to an audio file

Figure 16.14 Splitting a Part at M-Points

If you say Yes to Dynamic Time Compression, the program processes each section of the file to fit the timing of the source file. You might like to experiment with both methods, depending on the result you want. If Mac users have TimeBandit installed, this can be used to do the time stretching rather than VST. The option is set in the Preferences>Audio menu.

You can use this method to quantize one audio Part with another audio Part, too.

Importing Grooves from pre-v4 versions of Cubase
In previous versions of Cubase, Grooves were stored in a special file format containing all the Grooves. You can import these by selecting File>Import>Cubase 3.x Grooves. Each Groove will be converted and saved in a sub-folder.

Quantizing guitar recordings
Using a MIDI guitar controller for recording can present special problems when it comes to quantization. If the guitar parts have been strummed you're likely to have lots of short notes, very much off the beat which quantization is very likely to want to move.

It's extremely difficult to quantize such parts while retaining the same feel so the general advice is – don't! You may be able to adjust some notes manually but it's often better to record the part again.

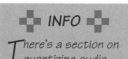

INFO

There's a section on quantizing audio Parts in Chapter 13. It ties in with several audio processing functions described in that chapter which makes it more suitable for inclusion there than here.

17

Files and file handling

Songs and Arrangements

These are two main file formats which you use for saving your music – Songs and Arrangements.

The Song format saves all the Arrangements, the Audio Pool, audio and dialog settings and, basically, the entire setup. On the PC, Song files have an .ALL extension and on the Mac the icons are stamped with SONG, Figure 17.1.

The Arrangement format saves what you see in the Arrange window. On the PC these files have an .ARR extension and on the Mac the icons are stamped with ARR, Figure 17.1. You can have up to 16 Arrangements in one Song. If you select Close on the File menu, a dialog appears which includes the option to Set Aside the Arrangement. This closes the window and 'hides' it from current view but it can be opened from the Windows>Arrangements menu.

It's important to note that Arrangements do not contain Audio Pool settings. It's also important to note that Song files do not save the audio data. Instead they reference the files so when a Song is loaded VST knows where to look for the files on your hard disk.

In order to save the maximum amount of information with your work, you should always save in Song format, even if it only contains one Arrangement. The only disadvantage is that Song files are larger than Arrangements files but this is generally of no consequence in these days of large and cheap hard disks.

Figure 17.1 On the Mac, Song and Arrangement file icons are stamped with their name

✿ **INFO** ✿

*T*here is no 'Close Song' command in VST and even if you close all the Arrangement windows the Song is still there. To create a new Song select 'New Song' from the File menu.

Other VST file formats

It's worth remembering that VST has several other file formats for storing specific items of data, Figure 17.2. You can use them to transfer individual parts of a Song, settings in VST or aspects of your configuration between Songs. The list includes:

Part	Contains MIDI or audio events. Audio Parts reference the audio on disk, they don't store the actually audio data.
Drum map	Settings for drum sounds.
Setup	General settings within VST.
Window Set	Snapshot of a Windows Set.

Keyboard layout	Custom set of Key Commands.
Score set	Various settings used in the Score editor, only available in VST Score and VST/24.
Stationery	These files are essentially like Song files but cannot be saved using the 'Save' function – you must use 'Save as'. Use them to create template files which you can't accidentally overwrite.

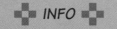

There's more about using Stationery files to create Autoload files and templates in Chapter 3.

Figure 17.2 VST file formats

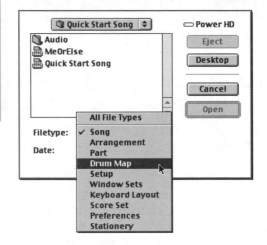

Transferring a Song to another computer

If your Song contains only MIDI data, you can simply copy the Song file and that's it.

However, if the Song contains audio data, you need to make sure that all the audio files are copied, too. There are two functions you can use to do this – Prepare Archive and Prepare Master, both available from the Audio Pool's File menu.

Prepare Archive copies all the files used in the Song (or all the files in the Audio Pool, even if they are not actually used in the Song) to a new folder. After selecting a folder, you are given the option to include Referenced (just the files used in the Song) or All files. The routine then copies the files, including the Song file, into the designated folder.

Prepare Master extracts only the portions of files used in the Song, stores them as new files and updates the Song. It is, therefore, much more compact. The process is non-destructive and does not erase any existing audio files.

Exchanging files with older versions of Cubase

VST can also import ReCycle files – great if you work with loops.

VST v4 can load files created with earlier versions of Cubase and it can also import files created by Pro-24, which was an early sequencer developed by Steinberg.

VST can also export files in both Song and Arrangement formats compatible with Cubase 3.x. Useful if you're collaborating with someone who hasn't upgraded yet...

Saving MIDI files

One the one hand, saving files in Standard MIDI File format is easy. On the other, there are several considerations to take into account.

To save a MIDI file, mute the Tracks you do not want to save with the file (audio Tracks are automatically excluded from this procedure), and select Export MIDI File from the File menu.

You may then get a dialog asking if you want to save the file in Format 0 or 1. Some versions of VST do not give you this option and automatically save MIDI files in Format 1. However, if you export a MIDI file with only one Track unmuted, it will create a Format 0 file.

To put all MIDI parts onto one Track, set the Left and Right Locators to the start and end of the section you want to save, select an empty Track and then select Merge Tracks from the Structure menu (in earlier versions of VST this may be Mix Down).

There is also an option in the Preference>MIDI>MIDI Files box to 'Include Part Parameters in Exported Files'. When this is on, any Part parameters set in the Inspector are converted to MIDI events and included in the file. But see the section on Freezing Parameters in Chapter 7 before you use this.

Backing up

After completing a project, mixing it down and creating a final copy on DAT or CD, you'll want to remove the files which have accumulated on your hard disk to free-up space for your next project. There ought to be a reluctance to throw them away because you never know when you may want to do a remix or a reworking of the piece. So you need to back them up.

As already described in this Chapter, VST itself can help archive material used in a song but you may also want to keep the bits not used in the song – out-takes, unused recordings, samples and so on.

The easiest and cheapest backup method is currently CD-R. These drives continue to fall in price as do blank CD-R discs which are cheaper than a Tube ticket for the Underground so for the minimal cost involved it seems churlish not to backup the entire project and associated files onto a CD.

There is some controversy over how long data on a CD will last when stored. You maybe like to browse the Web for current thinking on this but to make doubly sure, you could make two CD copies of the data.

You could, of course, backup the data using any other traditional computer archiving method or even backup the audio files to DAT, although if there are many this could be time-consuming and you have to retrieve them in a linear fashion.

INFO

Format 1 MIDI files put each MIDI channel on its own Track, and this is the preferred format for transferring files to another sequencer as it makes editing relatively easy. Format 0 files have the data for all MIDI channels on one Track. It may be necessary to use this format in order to play the files on some hardware sequencers, particularly those built into keyboards, and MIDI File Players.

18

Audio troubleshooting

No sound from audio output

This assumes that your system had been playing audio okay in the past but has suddenly stopped for some reason.

Before you start looking for problems within VST it's worth checking that all the audio and connecting cables are okay. It's easy to catch a wire and pull out a jack without noticing.

Check the audio outputs directly by plugging them into a set of headphones.

On the PC, if using a sound card, open the mixer (most sound card software includes a mixer application) and make sure the output is not muted and the volume is turned up.

On the Mac, if using the built-in sound, check the Sound and the Monitors & Sound Control Panel, Figure 18.1, to make sure the output is set to a suitable volume level and not muted.

Figure 18.1 Check that the audio volume is at a suitable level

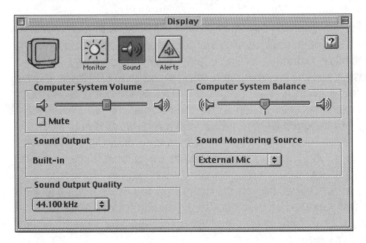

If you have recently installed some new software or experienced a severe crash, check that the sound card is still properly installed, and that the new software has not overwritten or replaced any drivers.

AWE64 Wave Guide conflict

The Creative Labs AWE64's Wave Guide Synth/WG driver conflicts with the digital audio system. It grabs the audio output so, consequently, VST cannot play any audio parts. You may get an error message saying that the audio system cannot be reached.

It needs to be disabled and to do so, reboot your computer and make sure no programs are running. Run the Setup MME program and look in the Outputs box for AWE MIDI Mapper and AWE64 Wave Guide Synth/WG. Select them in turn then click on the Set Inactive button. Try that.

If you still cannot record and playback simultaneously, launch the Creative Audio Mixer and switch on the LEDs with the Switch LED On button (lower right under the LED display), Figure 18.2. The first suggestion should work most in most cases but this suggestion comes from Steinberg Tech Support who offer it as a secondary fix.

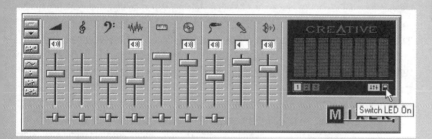

Figure 18.2 The Creative Audio Mixer

Playback quality is poor while recording

This is a common complaint with some of the Creative Labs AWE and Sound Blaster cards although it ceased with the release of the Live! card. The problem is a feature of the cards themselves and sometimes the drivers.

The AWE cards record at 16-bit but if you play back audio while recording they only playback at 8-bit so no wonder the playback quality sounds poor. However, most users find it quite adequate for monitoring and when you do play back (without recording) the audio plays at 16-bit.

The problem may also occur with other sound cards. It's simply the way the cards have been designed. Sometimes a new driver may fix the problem but if it's really giving you grief you may have to upgrade your card.

Multiple sound cards' outputs not in sync

If you have two or more audio cards in your PC you can use them all for playing back audio. However, they may not all play in sync.

The reason is that the clock rate of the card is used to synchronize MIDI and audio and as the clock rate on different cards may vary, even a little, it's possible for the audio to run out of sync.

If you really need multiple audio outs, the easiest solution, albeit one which costs money, is to invest in a multiple I/O card. Or you could arrange your recordings so everything is routed to a stereo mix and output through one sound card.

Audio drop outs

If the audio sometimes seems to disappear or go out of sync, there can be several causes.

Figure 18.3 The Audio
Performance Meter

Assuming your system has been working okay before, the most common cause of drop outs is that you're asking your computer system to do more that it's capable of. Pull up the Audio Performance meter, Figure 18.3, and check it during playback. If either of the meters light the Over LED, you're overtaxing your computer. Sometimes the LEDs flash briefly when you start or stop playback but providing playback begins okay, that's nothing to worry about.

The CPU meter can overload if you use too many real-time effects, too many EQ modules or try to play too many audio channels at once.

The Disk meter will overload if the disk is not able to transfer data quickly enough for the computer to play it. You can alleviate the strain by reducing the number of audio channels and increasing the Disk Block Buffer Size, which you can do in the Audio System Setup dialog, Figure 18.4.

Figure 18.4 Changing the Disk
Block Buffer Size may
improve performance

Try muting some Tracks and disabling real-time plug-ins. If this plays back okay, you're overtaxing your system.

Defragment your hard disk. This has been known to cure playback problems at a stroke, especially if there are lots of audio files in a piece, if the hard disk is quite full, or if files have been recorded and erased regularly. See Chapter 2 for more about defragmentation.

Switch off or disable all TSR (Terminate and Stay Resident) applications which run in the background. This includes networking, screen savers, task schedulers and utilities which monitor your computer's performance. They all take a share of CPU power which leaves less for VST. If they kick in to do a spot check, that could prove just too much for the system and cause a drop out.

On the Mac, switch off Virtual Memory in the Memory Control Panel. This should rarely be used with any program. If you're short of RAM, buy some more – it's quite cheap.

Make sure you have the latest drivers for your sound card. New drivers may fix bugs – yes, really! – and may even improve performance.

PC

Crackles and clicks

These can be caused by spikes in the audio data but some graphics cards, particularly S3-based cards for the PC, have been known to interfere with audio playback. Most of these problems have been sorted now. They were caused by the card hogging the PCI bus for a little longer than it should have done in order to boost video performance. Hogging the bus means the bus is not available to an audio card and this can cause glitching.

After this was discovered many manufacturers included an option in the card's setup panel, something like 'Power GDI Acceleration', which can be disabled to alleviate the problem. If you have such a card and you think it's causing problems, it's worth checking with the manufacturer for updated software.

Most graphics cards now have acceleration and occasionally this can cause problems, too. Typical symptoms include: crackles when the Arrange window is redrawn in Follow Song mode after the Song Position Pointer reaches the right hand edge of the window; crackles when you resize the screen; crackling when 16-, 24- or 32-bit colour modes are used; and crackling when the Transport, Monitor or Master windows are displayed.

If you experience any of these problems, try reducing the hardware acceleration in the Advanced dialog of the video Settings properties page, Figure 18.5.

Figure 18.5 Reducing a
graphic card's hardware
acceleration may prevent
crackles

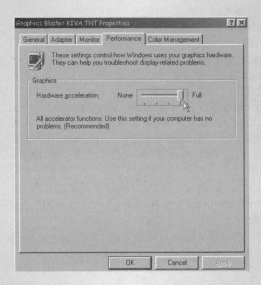

More graphics card problems
There are a few tests you can run to see if the graphics card is causing a
problem. Open an audio file, start playback then move and drop the window around the screen. If playback crackles or glitches or the audio swaps
channels, the video card could be the culprit.

If disabling Power GDI Acceleration and reducing hardware acceleration, described above, doesn't fix it, add the following lines to the
system.ini file:

[mga.drv]
PCIChipset=1

The easiest way to edit the system.ini file is with Sysedit. This may not
have been installed on your PC – use the Find facility to find out – but it's
on the Windows CD and can easily be copied to your hard disk.

With some graphics cards it may also help to reduce the number of
colours which you can do in the Display Control Panel under the Settings
Tab.

VST is unstable and has timing problems
These symptoms can occur in various degrees of severity for several reasons. It's essential that you setup the audio and MIDI sections of VST correctly. Refer to Chapter 1 and do read the instructions which come with
VST. In particular, if you are having problems with transferring data
between ADAT devices, you may need ASIO 2 drivers. See Chapter 1 for
more information about ASIO 2.

Check the suggestions in the Audio drop outs section above. If your computer is not up to speed, timing problems can occur because the computer can't keep up with the demands placed upon it.

Some versions of the Mac OS have been suspected of causing timing problems with VST. Check with your Steinberg distributor and on the Steinberg Web site to see if there are any adverse reports about the OS you are using.

Again on the Mac, OMS has been known to fix some MIDI timing problems.

Make sure you have enough RAM. 64Mb ought to be regarded as a minimum. Insufficient RAM can cause the computer to write files to disk which can slow it down.

Switch Autosave off.

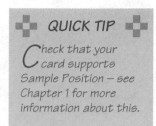

QUICK TIP

Check that your card supports Sample Position – see Chapter 1 for more information about this.

If timing still seems a little shaky, you can try setting Virtual Memory to a fixed amount. This seems to be another of those sometimes-it-works/ sometimes-it-doesn't things where some users report an improvement in performance and others don't. The setting is found in the System Control Panel under Performance>Virtual Memory, Figure 18.6. The recommended setting for most applications is to let Windows manage its own VM settings. It can then use as much or a little disk space as it requires.

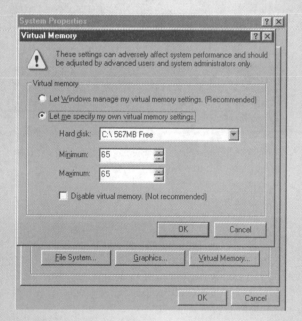

Figure 18.6 Adjusting Virtual Memory may improve performance – or it may not!

This recommendation is to set the Minimum and Maximum amounts to the same size, somewhere between 50Mb and 250Mb. In an EIDE system it should be on the boot drive; if you have a SCSI drive, use that, but do not use the drive dedicated to recording digital audio. If you get an Out of Memory error with this setting, you need to increase the size of the VM allocation. After setting it up, defragment the drive.

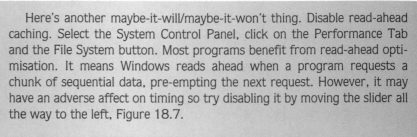

Here's another maybe-it-will/maybe-it-won't thing. Disable read-ahead caching. Select the System Control Panel, click on the Performance Tab and the File System button. Most programs benefit from read-ahead optimisation. It means Windows reads ahead when a program requests a chunk of sequential data, pre-empting the next request. However, it may have an adverse affect on timing so try disabling it by moving the slider all the way to the left, Figure 18.7.

Figure 18.7 Read-ahead optimisation may improve performance

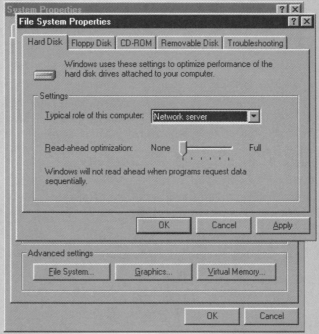

Also, set the 'Typical role of this computer' to network server which ought to give better audio performance.

This may be something of a rarity but it's worth mentioning. Some timing problems have been traced to combinations of motherboards and BIOSs (mostly Award) in combination with UDMA hard drives. UDMA should bypass the CPU leaving it free for other tasks but it has been known to grab the ISA bus causing timing problems with ISA cards. If you have a combination of equipment which you think may be causing a problem, here's a fix to try:

While booting your PC hold down the DEL key to enter the BIOS configuration set-up. Select 'PnP and PCI Setup' or 'PnP Configuration'. There should be a setting which reads' PCI IDE IRQ Mapped to:' which is usually set to 'PCI Auto'. Change this to 'ISA' or 'Legacy ISA'. Save the changes, exit and restart. Hopefully, that will cure it.

BUT FIRST A WARNING
Be very careful when messing with the BIOS settings. An inadvertent change here or there could completely screw your machine so don't mess with the BIOS unless you know what you're doing and follow the above suggestions at your own risk.

There. I feel better now.

Audio and MIDI Tracks run out of sync
First of all, try everything mentioned above!

Don't start the song at bar 1. Leave a blank bar to give VST time to 'get rolling' and start the song at bar 2.

Put a bar of empty audio at the start of the piece so the audio kicks in before the MIDI parts.

Adjust the MIDI to Audio Delay setting in the Audio System Setup dialog, Figure 18.8. Positive values will delay MIDI playback. This may help if MIDI parts seem to be constantly behind or ahead of the audio.

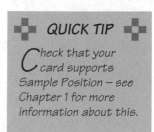

QUICK TIP

Check that your card supports Sample Position – see Chapter 1 for more information about this.

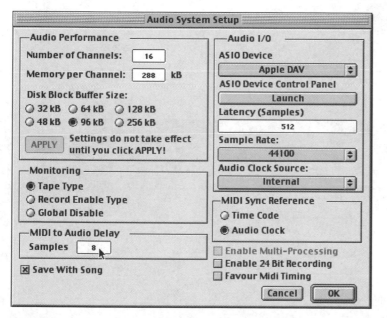

Figure 18.8 Adjusting MIDI to Audio Delay can improve sync problems

MAC

The Audio System Setup dialog also has a Favour MIDI Timing option which gives MIDI processing a higher priority than audio processing. Check this if using OMS but make sure the CPU Over indicator in the Audio Performance window doesn't light up.

Problems can sometimes be caused by Preroll being less than the Latency figure. To set up Preroll correctly, open the Audio System dialog and look at the Latency figure which is below the ASIO Control Panel button, Figure 18.9. Then, in the Options>Synchronization menu, change the System Preroll to equal this figure, Figure 18.10. If this doesn't fix it, try setting the Preroll figure to a slightly higher value.

Figure 18.9 Check the latency figure

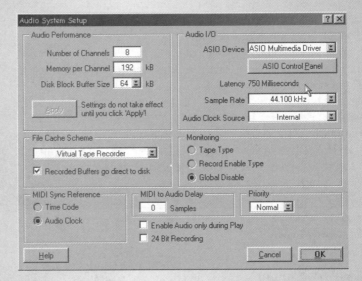

Figure 18.10 Set Preroll to equal or slightly exceed the latency value

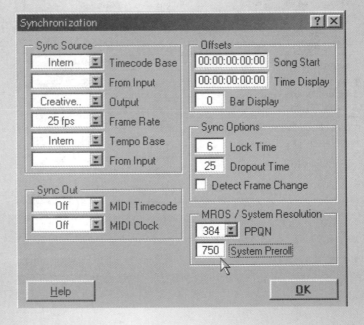

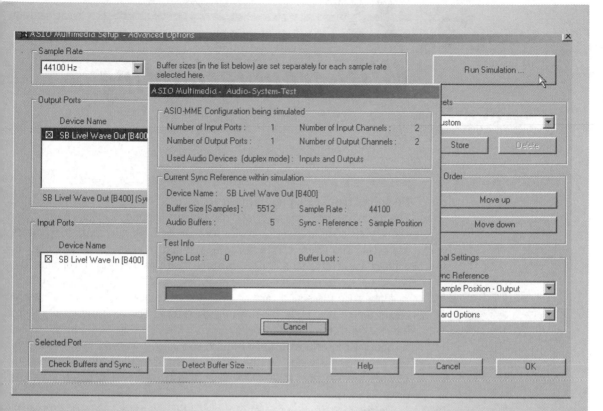

Do use the Run Simulation option in the Advanced section of the Multimedia Setup dialog, Figure 18.11, which tests the sound card's configuration.

Figure 18.11 Run Simulation checks the sound card's configuration

VST just stops recording

The most common cause of this problem is the hard disk. Make sure the hard disk is defragmented, that all TSR programs are disabled and that there is enough free space on the disk for the audio you want to record.

It's also worth checking the system optimisation suggestions above, too.

MIDI troubleshooting

No sound from MIDI equipment

The most common source of audio problems is dodgy cabling. Before you blame your computer setup, make sure all the MIDI and connecting cables are okay. Try direct connections. If a sound module is not responding, connect it directly to a MIDI keyboard (without routing it through the computer system) and check that it works.

Make sure the sound card or MIDI interface are correctly installed and connected to the sound module/keyboard/serial port or otherwise able to interface with the outside world.

Specialist interfaces usually require specialist drivers so make sure they are correctly installed. On the PC open the Control Panel>Multimedia> Devices tab, expand MIDI Devices and Instruments and make sure the driver is there.

On the Mac, if you are using Apple's MIDI Manager, OMS or FreeMIDI, make sure it is correctly installed and set-up. Setting up OMS, for example, can be a little involved so read the manual carefully.

On the PC, if using a sound card, open the mixer (most sound card software includes a mixer application) and make sure the output is not muted and the volume is turned up.

On the PC, it's possible that there could be an IRQ conflict with the sound card. Windows 98 and the Plug 'n' Play system, although not foolproof, should ensure that this rarely happens but you might want to check it out anyway. In Control Panel>System>Device Manager, double click on the Computer icon at the top of the list to view the devices by IRQ, I/O and DMA settings, Figure 19.1. This will enable you to check if there are any conflicts. If there are, refer to the hardware's instructions for changing them. You may be able to do it via software but some devices require you to change jumpers on the card itself.

Playback volume suddenly drops

This is a surprisingly common occurrence among people who use the Inspector although v4 has made it a little more difficult to do. It often occurs when fiddling with the Volume parameter. If you take this down to a low value, say down to 0, the value is transmitted to the MIDI instrument and consequently all subsequent notes play at zero volume.

Try resetting the synth or sound module, inserting a starting volume in the MIDI data or setting the Volume parameters in the Inspector to 127.

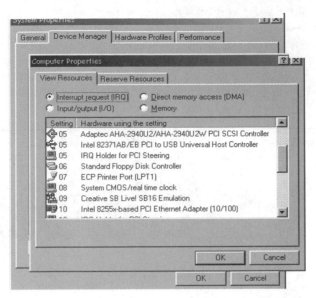

Figure 19.1 Check the Device Manager to make sure there are no conflicts

It's more difficult to inadvertently run the Volume value through zero in v4 because when you click on the Volume parameter a slider pops up which you can easily adjust to any value. In previous versions of VST you had to scroll through a Volume value and it was easy to stop just before the Off setting, causing a very low volume value to be sent to the synth.

Pitch bend sounds wrong

You play a piece of music and the material obviously has some pitch bend data in it but the bend doesn't sound right – it's either not enough or completely OTT. This can happen when the pitch bend range of the recording instrument is different to that of the receiving instrument. Most instruments have a facility which enables you to set their pitch bend range. A common setting is one octave but some users may prefer something more modest such as four or five semitones.

If you dig around inside your synth's settings you should find a parameter which lets you set the pitch bend range. You can probably also set this via MIDI messages.

If you have a GM instrument, the following list of data can be entered in the List editor to set the pitch bend range:

Controller 101	0	RPN MSB
Controller 100	0	RPN LSB
Controller 6	12	Set pitch bend to 12 semitones
Controller 101	127	RPN MSB
Controller 100	127	RPN LSB

You can vary the middle value to change the pitch bend range.

Pitch bend or modulation goes doolally after merging parts

If you merge parts which contain Controller data, that data will be merged, too. Particularly with pitch bend and modulation, this can cause all sorts of anomalies. Merging a note containing an upward bend with a note which contains a downward bend could result in neither of them bending correctly. The most common result of injudicious merging is a jump in the modulation data.

Figure 19.2 shows two parts containing an upward and a downward bend, and the result of merging them. It's an exaggerated example, but it shows how disastrous this could be when applied to notes.

Figure 19.2 A cautionary – if somewhat exaggerated – tale of the potential hazards of merging data

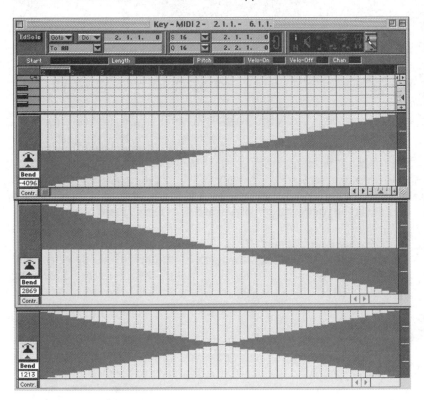

To avoid this – don't merge the parts and keep them on separate MIDI channels. Alternatively, remove the least-important data from one of the parts so the other modulation works correctly.

Double notes

If you hear double notes when you play your keyboard, a little like slap-back echo or flanging, the chances are you have not got MIDI Thru in VST and Local Control on your keyboard set up correctly. This causes the keyboard to sound two notes – the one you play on the keyboard and another being echoed from your computer. See the Thru and Thru section (page 15 in Chapter 3) for information about how to set these up to avoid this.

Stuck notes – the dreaded MIDI drone

Most users will have experienced the dreaded MIDI drone – a stuck note which switches on but which doesn't switch off. It happens when a synth receives a Note On message but doesn't receive a corresponding Note Off message. It can happen for a number of reasons.

- If a synth receives more data than it can process – a situation commonly referred to as MIDI Clog or Choke – some instructions may be lost. If it's a Note Off message, a stuck note will result. If this is a repeatable problem with a synth, you're feeding it too much data. If there is a lot of Controller data at the stuck note point, try thinning it down. You can do this with Functions>MIDI Functions>Reduce Cont. Data, Figure 19.3.
- Variations on the above include trying to transmit more data than MIDI is capable of handling. The situation can often be resolved by using an additional MIDI interface or a MIDI Thru box instead of daisy chaining instruments.
- Stuck notes can occur if you change MIDI channel during playback – an instrument receives a Note On message on one channel but you change the transmit channel before the Note Off message has been sent. Uh oh...

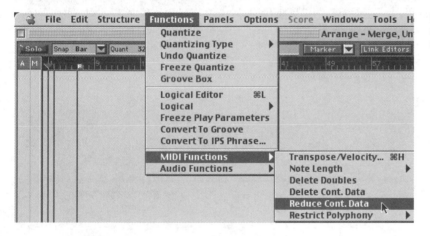

Figure 19.3 If stuck notes are a problem try thinning controller data

You can stop the drone by using the Reset Devices command in VST's Option menu. When this is selected, VST sends messages to reset pitch bend, modulation and pressure. A Reset All Controllers message is sent along with an All Notes Off message and it resets all connected MIDI devices such as MIDI interface and synchronization devices.

Synth sounds strange at the high and low ends of the scale

Not all instruments support MIDI's full 128-note range. You can check the range they respond to in their MIDI Implementation Chart (in the manual) and this may tell you what happens if it receives messages outside its range. Some 'fold back' the notes so they play at the highest or lowest octave the instrument supports. Others may ignore notes outside their range and a few may produce strange sounds, although this happens rarely with modern instruments.

Appendix 1
Key Commands

The sure-fire tell-tale sign of a power user is one who uses the computer keyboard more than the mouse – all the hackers on TV and in the movies never use the mouse!

The main reason is that using the keyboard to select a function is far quicker than using the mouse. Learn one or two new Key Commands each day – or even each week – and you'll soon become an expert.

The following lists of Key Commands are the default settings which apply to the current versions of VST as we went to print. The vast majority are likely to remain unchanged, although it's possible that Steinberg may alter a few as changes or new features are added to the program.

In certain versions of VST you can define your own Key Commands but be wary of doing so for two reasons:

1 A great many key combinations are already used, particularly the more obvious ones, and unless you're careful and well organised you run the risk of redefining existing Commands which could cause confusion, and
2 If it's likely that you will use copies of VST on other computers or other VST users may use yours, changing the default Key Commands will cause a lot of confusion.

Mac Key Commands

File menu

Key Command	Function
Command N	New arrangement
Command O	Open
Command S	Save
Command P	Print (in Score or List edit only)
Command Q	Quit

Edit menu

Key Command	Function
Command Z	Undo
Command X	Cut
Command C	Copy
Command V	Paste
Command A	Select all parts/events
Command I	Get info
Command E	Open Key edit or default editor (depending on Track Class)
Command G	Open List edit window
Command D	Open Drum editor
Command R	Open Score editor
Command M	Open Graphic MasterTrack window
Command B	Open Notepad window

Structure menu

Key Command	Function
Command T	Create Track
Command P	Create Part
Command K	Repeat Parts
Command J	Show Groups
Command U	Build Group

Functions menu

Key Command	Function
Q	Quantize
U	Undo quantize
Command L	Open Logical editor
Command H	Transpose/Velocity
Command T	Fixed length

Panels Menu

Key Command	Function
Command {Num *]	Open Audio Channel Mixer
Command [Num +]	Open Audio Master window
Command [Num =]	Audio Send Effects
Command [Num /]	Audio Master Effects
Command F	Open Audio Pool

Options menu

Key Command	Function
F	Follow song
Command Y	Ears only

Score menu

Key Command	Function
Option 1-8	Move to Voice 1-8
Option X	Flip
Option G	Group
Option B	Hide

Arrange/editors

Key Command	Function
Command 1-9	Select Tool 1-9
Space	Alternate Stop key
Option L	Set left loop
Option R	Set right loop
Option C	Controller Display On/Off
Option P	Locator to selected parts
Option I	Note info
Option M	Mute selected Track

Arrange/editors (continued)

Key Command	Function
Option O	Loop On/Off
Option N	Name drum
Option J	Name instrument
Option W	IPS On/Off
Option S	Drum solo
A	Editor solo
X	Sync On/Off
C	Click On/Off
S	Solo On/Off
L	Edit left Locator
R	Edit right Locator
P	Edit position
I	Punch In On/Off
O	Punch Out On/Off
M	Master On/Off
V	Cycle Rec: Delete Last
B	Cycle Rec: Delete Subtrack
N	Cycle Rec: Quantize Last
K	Cycle Rec: Key Erase
1	Quantize to whole note
2	Quantize to half note
3	Quantize to quarter note
4	Quantize to eighth note
5	Quantize to 16th note
6	Quantize to 32nd note
7	Quantize to 64th note
8	Quantize to 128th note
T	Quantize to triplet On/Off
.	Quantize to Dotted On/Off
Shift H	Zoom in vertical
H	Zoom in horizontal

Arrange/editors (continued)

Key Command	Function
Shift G	Zoom out vertical
G	Zoom out horizontal
Y	Remote On/Off
Z	Auto quantize On/Off
Page Up	Last page
Page Down	Next page
Numlock	Rewind
Shift Numlock	Fast Rewind
[Num =]	Forward
Shift [Num =]	Fast Forward
[Num 0]	Stop
[Num Enter]	Start
[Num *]	Record
[Num –}	Tempo down
[Num +]	Tempo up
[Num /]	Cycle
[Num 1]	Position to left Locator
Shift [Num 1]	Left Locator to position
[Num 2]	Position to right Locator
Shift [Num 2]	Right Locator to position
[Num 3] to [Num 9]	Recall Locator 1 – 7
Shift [Num 3] to [Num 9]	Store Locator 1 – 7
Shift 1 – 0	Recall Mutes 1 – 10
Shift Option 1 – 0	Program Mutes 1 – 10
Command 1 – 0	Recall Locators 1 – 10
Command Option 1 – 0	Program Locators 1 – 10

PC Key Commands

The PC Keyboard Commands are grouped according to their context.

Numeric keypad

Numeric keypad commands

Key Command	Function
*	Activate recording
Enter	Start/Continue
0 or Spacebar	1st time: Stop 2nd time: Go to left Locator/1.1.0 3rd time: Go to 1.1.0
+	Increase tempo
–	Decrease tempo
1	Go to Left Locator
2	Go to Right Locator
9	Go to last Stop Position
Shift 1	Store Song Position as Left Locator
Shift 2	Store Song Position as Right Locator
3 to 8	Go to Cue Point 3 to 8
Shift 3 to 8	Store Song Position as Cue Point 3 to 8
/	Cycle On/Off

Typewriter keyboard

File handling and general procedures

Key Command	Function
Control O	Open
Shift Control N	New Song
Control S	Save Song
Shift Control S	Save Arrangement
Control Z	Undo
Control X	Cut
Control C	Copy
Control V	Paste
Control Q	Quit

Window handling

Key Command	Function
Control N	New Arrange window
Control W	Close active window
Return	Close editor or 'click button with bold label' in Dialog Box
Esc	Close and Cancel in Dialog Boxes
G	Decrease horizontal magnification
H	Increase horizontal magnification
Shift G	Decrease vertical magnification
Shift H	Increase vertical magnification
F12	Hide/Show Transport Bar
Shift F12	Hide/Show VST Windows
Control F12	Bring VST Windows to front
Control E	Open Key edit or default editor (depending on Track Class)
Control G	Open List edit window
Control R	Open Score edit window
Control L	Open Logical edit window
Control Y	Open GM/GS/XG editor
Control F	Open Audio Pool window
Control [keypad *]	Open Audio Monitor Mixer
Control [keypad +]	Open Audio Master window
Control M	Open Graphic Master Track window
Shift Control M	Open Master Track List
Control H	Open Transpose/Velocity dialog
Control B	Open Notepad window
F1	Open Online Help

Transport Bar functions

Key Command	Function
Page Up	Forward
Page Down	Rewind
P	Set Meter Position
Shift P	Set Time Position
Shift T	Set Tempo
Shift S	Set Time Signature
L	Set Left Locator
R	Set Right Locator
Alt Control P	Set Left and Right Locator to Part's Start and End
Shift F2 to F11	Store Locator settings
F2 to F11	Recall Locator settings
C	Click On/Off
D	Toggle Record Mode (Overdub/Replace)
F	Follow Song On/Off
I	Punch In On/Off
O	Punch Out On/Off
M	Master Track On/Off
S	Solo On/Off
X	Sync On/Off
Y	Remote On/Off
V	Delete last version (MIDI Cycle Recording)
B	Delete Subtrack (MIDI Cycle Recording)
N	Quantize last version (MIDI Cycle Recording)
K	Key Erase (MIDI Cycle Recording)

General selection and editing

Key Command	Function
Control A	Select All Parts/Events
Backspace	Delete Selection
Control Backspace	Permanently delete audio from the hard disk
Control I	Get Information about selected Parts/elements
Q	Over Quantize
U	Undo Quantize
W	Note On Quantize
E	Iterative Quantize
J	Groove Quantize
Z	Auto Quantize On/Off
1 to 7	Set Quantize value
T	Set Quantize value to triplets
.	Set Quantize value to dotted

Arrange Window selection and editing

Key Command	Function
[Right cursor key]	Select Next Part
[Left cursor key]	Select Previous Part
[Up cursor key]	Go one Track up
[Down cursor key]	Go one Track down
Control T	Create Track
Alt Control T	Select Track (enter a Track number, counted from the top of the Track list)
Alt Control N	Rename Track
Alt Control C	Set MIDI/Audio Channel for selected Track
Alt Control O	Set MIDI Output for selected Track
Alt Control J	Create/Rename Instrument for selected Track
Shift Control T	Set Track Class for selected Track (enter a number 1 – 7, corresponding to the order on the Track Class pop-up menu)
Alt Control M	Monitoring On/Off (Audio Track) / Mute On/Off (others)
Shift Alt Control F2 to F11	Store Mute settings

Arrange Window selection and editing (continued)

Key Command	Function
Alt Control F2 to F11	Recall Mute settings
Control P	Create Part
Control K	Repeat Part(s)
Alt Control A	Toggle Part Appearance between 'Show Names' and 'Show Events'
Alt Control I	Open/Close Inspector
Shift O	Edit Transpose (in Inspector)
Shift V	Edit Velocity (in Inspector)
Shift D	Edit Delay (in Inspector)
Alt Control F	Freeze Play Parameters
Control J	Show/Hide Groups
Control U	Build Group

All MIDI editor windows

Key Command	Function
Return	Keep (Close editor, keeping changes)
Esc	Cancel (Close editor, discarding changes)
Insert	Insert Event
Tab	Move one Snap in Step Edit
A	Edit Solo On/Off
Alt Control O	Loop On/Off
Alt Control L	Input Left Loop boundary
Alt Control R	Input Right Loop boundary
Alt Control I	Info On/Off
Alt Control C	Show/Hide Controller display

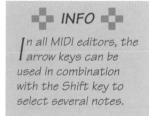

INFO

In all MIDI editors, the arrow keys can be used in combination with the Shift key to select several notes.

Key edit only

Key Command	Function
Alternate	Restrict Pen to length changes only
[Right cursor key]	Next Note
[Left cursor key]	Previous Note

Drum edit only

Key Command	Function
[Right cursor key]	Next Note
[Left cursor key]	Previous Note
[Up cursor key]	Previous Sound
[Down cursor key]	Next Sound
Alt Control S	Solo On/Off (for selected Sound)
Alt Control N	Rename Sound

Score edit only

Key Command	Function
[Right cursor key]	Next Note
[Left cursor key]	Previous Note
[Up cursor key]	Next Staff
[Down cursor key]	Previous Staff
Control + Cursor key	Move selected item up/down/left/right
+ (Typewriter Keyboard)	Move Tablature note one string up
– (Typewriter Keyboard)	Move Tablature note one string down
Alt Control X	Flip Stems
Alt Control G	Group selected items
Alt Control B	Hide selected items
Alt Control H	Grace Note
Alt Control 1 – 8	To Voice 1 – To Voice 8
Control P	Print Score

List edit only

Key Command	Function
[Up cursor key]	Previous Event
[Down cursor key]	Next Event

Pool functions

Key Command	Function
Alt Control N	Rename Segment

MIDI Mixer Window only

Key Command	Function
[Up cursor key]	Increase Object Value
[Down cursor key]	Decrease Object Value
Control I	Open Object Dialog Box

Appendix 2
Tools summary

In order to get the best out of Cubase, you need to be familiar with the Tools. These vary slightly from editor to editor and their function can vary slightly, too, between editors. Here's a brief summary of the Tools and the functions they perform in the editors. A full list of all the Tools' functions is available in the VST documentation.

Arrange

Arrow
Used to select, move and copy Parts

Pencil
Can create a new Part, and change the length and starting point of a Part.

Eraser
Deletes a Part or selected Parts.

Scissors
Split a Part or Parts.

Speaker
Monitor the contents of an audio Part.

Glue Tube
Join a Part to other Parts.

Selection Range
Allows you to make a selection independent of the Parts. In other words, you don't have to select a complete Part.

Mute
Toggle Mute on and off by clicking on a Part.

Magnifying Glass
Click once to zoom in, drag to zoom in on an area.

Volume
Enables you to adjust the volume of a Part by clicking on it and then dragging on the slider which appears.

Pan
Click and drag the pop-up slider to change the Pan setting.

Transpose
Click and drag on the pop-up keyboard to transpose a Part.

Match Quantize
Drag one Part on top of another to copy its 'Groove' to the second Part.

Logical
Applies a Logical Preset to a Part. Clicking opens a pop-up menu of the presets.

Groove
Applies a Groove to a Part. Clicking opens a pop-up menu of the settings.

Stretch
Stretches (or shrinks) a Part and scales the events accordingly. For MIDI Parts the events are moved so the relative distance between them is the same. Audio Parts are time stretched.

Audio Edit

Arrow
Used for selecting, moving and duplicating events.

Pencil
Import an audio file by clicking into a free area and selecting a file from the dialogue box. It can also edit Volume and Pan curves, and Match Points when 'Dynamic events' is selected in the View pop-up menu.

Eraser
Deletes events, Volume/Pan breakpoints and Match Points.

Scissors
Split a file into two.

Speaker
Allows you to playback and scrub through audio events.

Crossfade
Used to define areas to crossfade between.

Hand
Moves events one Snap value in either direction.

Mute
Mutes and unmutes an event.

Key, List and Drum editors

Arrow
Used to select, move and duplicate events.

Pencil
This is only in the Key and List editors. It can be used to add notes and change their length. In the List editor, in conjunction with the Insert menu, it can insert events. In the Controller Display it can edit or create Continuous Controller data.

Drum Stick
This is only in the Drum editor. It works much like the Pencil in the other editors except that clicking on an existing note deletes it.

Eraser
Deletes one or more events by clicking or dragging.

Paint Brush
Draws in notes by dragging.

Speaker
Click on an event to play it, drag over several events to play them all.

Line
In the Note Display, draw a line over notes to make them shorter. In the Controller Display use it to draw in Controller ramps.

Kicker
Shifts or kicks an event by the Snap value in the direct the Kicker is pointing. On the Mac, press Option to change the direction of the kick.

Mute
Mute and unmute events by clicking on them.

Score Edit (non-Score versions of VST)

Arrow
Used to select, move and duplicate notes.

Text
Used to add text to the score.

Eraser
Deletes notes.

Scissors
Click on the second of a pair of tied notes to split them.

Speaker
Click on a note or drag over several notes to play them back.

Glue Tube
Click on a note to join it to the next note of the same pitch.

Note
Used to add new notes and change note lengths.

Rest
Inserts a rest into the score. It differs from the Note Tool by *inserting* rests, pushing notes following them to a later position.

Score Edit (Score versions of VST)

Arrow
Used to select, move and duplicate notes and objects.

Layout
Used to move notes and symbols visually without affecting the way they playback via MIDI. It is only available in Page Mode.

Eraser
Deletes notes and objects.

Scissors
Click on the second of a pair of tied notes to split them.

Speaker
Click on a note or drag over several notes to play them back

Glue Tube
Click on a note to join it to the next note of the same pitch.

Note
Used to add new notes and change note lengths.

Rest
Inserts a rest into the score. It differs from the Note Tool by *inserting* rests, pushing notes following them to a later position.

Cut Flag
Inserts an event which allows you to override the automatic handling and display of tied notes.

Kicker
Moves an event in the direction that the Kicker is pointing. On the Mac, press Option to change the direction of the kick.

Display Quantize
Adds display quantize to specific parts of the score.

Magnifying Glass
Click once to zoom in, drag to zoom in on an area.

Controller editor

Arrow
This is used mainly for selecting events.

Eraser
Delete one or more events by clicking and dragging.

Pencil
Used to edit or create 'continuous' events.

Line
Used to draw Controller ramps.

MIDI Mixer

Arrow
Used to select, move and duplicate Mixer objects.

Play
Used to 'play' objects to make them transmit MIDI data.

 Eraser Left
The Eraser Tools are used to delete recorded mixes created with the object you click on. This one deletes everything from the current Song Position to the end of the Part.

 Eraser Right
Deletes everything from the beginning of the Part up to the current Song Position.

 Eraser Between
Deletes everything in the Part and between the Left and Right Locators.

Graphical Master Track

 Arrow
Used for selecting, moving and duplicating events.

  Speaker
Can be used for auditioning audio if the Graphical Master Track is opened using 'Match Audio and Tempo'.

 Eraser
Click on or drag over events to delete them.

 Pencil
Used to change and insert tempo events, and insert Hitpoints and Time Signature events.

 Line
Used to create tempo ramps.

 Scissors
Used to cut apart connected Hitpoints.

 Kicker Left
Moves an event to the left by the Snap value.

 Kicker Right
Moves an event to the right by the Snap value.

Appendix 3
Useful contacts

Software and plug-ins

Antares
UK (Unity Audio): 01440 785843
USA: 408 399 0008
http://www.antarestech.com

Arbiter Pro MIDI
UK: 0181 970 1924

Arboretum
UK (Unity Audio): 01440 785843
USA: 650 738 4750
http://www.arboretum.com

Digidesign
UK: 01753 653322
USA: 650 842 7900
http://www.digidesign.com

DUY
UK (Syco): 0171 6256070
Spain: (+34) 932 174 510
http://www.duy.com

Lexicon
UK (Stirling Audio): 0171 624 6000
USA: 781 280 0300
http://www.lexicon.com

Sonic Foundry
UK (SCV London): 0171 9231892
USA: 608 256 3133
http://www.sonicfoundry.com

TC Works
UK (Arbiter): 0181 970 1924
USA: 805 373 1828
http://www.tcworks.de

Waves
UK (SCV London): 0171 9231892
USA: 423 689 5395
Israel: 972 3 510 7667
http://www.waves.com

Yamaha
UK: 01908 369254
USA: 714 522 9011
http://www.yamaha.co.uk

MIDI file suppliers

Hands On MIDI Software
UK: 01705 783100
USA: 818 347 9803
http://www.hands-on-midi.com

Heavenly Music
UK: 01255 821039
http://www.ortiz.demon.co.uk

Keyfax
UK: 01491 413938
USA: 408 688 4505
http://www.keyfax.com

MIDI Magic
UK: 01792 581123
http://websites.ntl.com/~midimagic

Sample CDs

Heavenly Music
UK: 01255 821039
http://www.ortiz.demon.co.uk

Keyfax
UK: 01491 413938
USA: 408 688 4505
http://www.keyfax.com

Time+Space
UK: 01837 841100
http://www.timespace.com

Sound cards and interfaces

Creamware
UK: 01667 451123
USA: 604 435 0540
Germany: 2241 5958 0
http://www.creamware.com

Creative Labs
UK: 01245 265265
http://www.creative.com

Digidesign
UK: 01753 653322
USA: 650 842 7900
http://www.digidesign.com

Digital Audio Labs
UK (Et Cetera): 01706 228039
USA: 612 559 9098
http://www.digitalaudio.com

Event
UK (Key Audio): 01245 344001
USA: 805 566 9993
http://www.event1.com

Guillemot
UK: 0181 944 9000
USA: 877 484 5536
http://www.guillemot.com

Korg
UK: 01908 857130
http://www.korg.com

Lexicon
UK (Stirling Audio): 0171 624 6000
USA: 781 280 0300
http://www.lexicon.com

Midiman
UK: 01309 671301
USA: 626 445 2842
http://www.midiman.net

Opcode
UK (SCV London): 0171 9231892
USA: 650 429 2400
http://www.opcode.com

Soundscape
UK: 01222 450120
USA: 805 658 7375
http://www.soundscape-digital.com

Terratec
UK: 01600 772111
USA: 949 487 3774
http://www.terratec.net

Turtle Beach
UK (Et Cetera): 01706 219999
USA: 1 800 233 9377
http://www.tbeach.com

Yamaha
UK: 01908 369254
USA: 714 522 9011
http://www.yamaha.co.uk

Useful web sites

Club Cubase
http://www.clubcubase.com
Independent Cubase User Group

CWU
http://www.studio201.com/cwu/
Cubase for Windows Users

PC Publishing
http://www.pc-publishing.co.uk
Publisher of extremely fine hi tech music
books

Propeller Head
http://propellerheads.se
ReBirth

Steinberg main German site
http://www.steinberg.de
Includes an English version

Steinberg UK site
http://dspace.dial.pipex.com/steinberg-uk/

Steinberg USA
http://www.steinberg-us.com

Index